Embracing Adult SEL

Social emotional learning (SEL) is frequently taught in schools, but how can educators embrace it in their own lives? In this helpful guidebook, Wendy Turner demonstrates the importance of SEL being embraced, understood, and modeled by all members of the learning community. First, she offers tools to increase your self-awareness, including mindset, identity and culture, strengths, and core values. Second, she shows what self-management is and why it matters in helping everyone manage complex emotions in myriad ways. Then she explains what empathy is, and is not, and how it pertains to social issues, identity, and culture. Next, she discusses relationships—how we can foster successful relationships with everyday tools to ignite and support positive connections. Finally, she shows how to synthesize our skills, improving decision-making and modeling this for our students. Throughout each chapter, she provides creative, easy-to-implement ideas, stories, and reflection questions so you can make the ideas your own, enabling you to authentically grow and thrive on your personal and professional path.

Wendy Turner is an experienced elementary educator in Wilmington, DE and has tremendous passion for and expertise in social emotional learning (SEL). Wendy was named the 2017 Delaware Teacher of the Year after six years in the classroom and has received numerous awards and recognition for her work after changing careers to become a teacher at age 40. These include the Presidential Award for Excellence Teaching Science, an NEA Foundation Global Learning Fellowship, and the NEA Educator Excellence Award as well as being named an Outstanding STEM Educator and a Compassion Champion in her home state of Delaware. Wendy is a thought leader on SEL, regularly contributing to blogs, articles, and podcasts on SEL. She is an experienced facilitator of professional development both locally and nationally.

Also Available from Routledge Eye On Education
(www.routledge.com/k-12)

First Aid for Teacher Burnout: How You Can Find Peace and Success
Jenny Grant Rankin

Mindfulness for Students: A Curriculum for Grades 3-8
Wendy Fuchs

The Flexible SEL Classroom: Practical Ways to Build Social Emotional Learning
Amber Chandler

Movie Magic in the Classroom: Ready-to-Use Guide for Teaching SEL
Amber Chandler

Pause, Ponder, and Persist in the Classroom: How Teachers Turn Challenges into Opportunities for Impact
Julie Schmidt Hasson

Embracing Adult SEL

An Educator's Guide to Personal Social Emotional Learning Success

Wendy Turner

Designed cover image: © Getty

First published 2024
by Routledge
605 Third Avenue, New York, NY 10158, USA

and by Routledge
4 Park Square, Milton Park, Abingdon, Oxon, OX14 4RN, UK

Routledge is an imprint of the Taylor & Francis Group, an informa business.

© 2024 Wendy Turner

The right of Wendy Turner to be identified as author of this work has been asserted in accordance with sections 77 and 78 of the Copyright, Designs and Patents Act 1988.

All rights reserved. No part of this book may be reprinted or reproduced or utilised in any form or by any electronic, mechanical, or other means, now known or hereafter invented, including photocopying and recording, or in any information storage or retrieval system, without permission in writing from the publishers.

Trademark notice: Product or corporate names may be trademarks or registered trademarks, and are used only for identification and explanation without intent to infringe.

ISBN: 978-1-032-60406-0 (hbk)
ISBN: 978-1-032-59252-7 (pbk)
ISBN: 978-1-003-45896-8 (ebk)

DOI: 10.4324/9781003458968

Typeset in Palatino
by SPi Technologies India Pvt Ltd (Straive)

For Team Turner. Dan, Maggie, and Mike. Thank you for accepting and supporting me, unconditionally, as I am. You inspire and motivate me beyond measure. I love you all so much. And for teachers. You are so much more than educators in so many ways the world will never know. I see you. Thank you for the extraordinary work you do.

Contents

Meet the Author	viii
Foreword by Pete Hall	x
Introduction: My Social Emotional Learning Journey	1
1 Understanding SEL: Where Are You on the Road to SEL Success?	10
2 Establishing Your Adult SEL Practice: Embrace Proactive, Reactive, and Reflective Practices	33
3 Leaning Into Ourselves: Start Your SEL Journey with Self-Awareness	48
4 Managing Ourselves Matters: Learn, Practice, and Model Self-Management	77
5 Moving from Self to Others: Empathy is Curious, Connected, and Active	103
6 Relationship Skills Matter: Grow Connections with Everyday Practices	124
7 Synthesizing Your SEL Skills: Powerful Decision-Making	148
8 Living Your Best SEL Life: Embrace SEL with Your Whole Self	166
References	185

Meet the Author
Wendy Turner

A true champion for social emotional learning (SEL), Wendy Turner is an experienced, passionate, and award-winning educator. After changing careers at age 40, she was honored as the Delaware Teacher of the Year in 2017, after six years in the classroom. Wendy honed her skills teaching elementary students at Mt. Pleasant Elementary School in Wilmington, Delaware for 12 years, 11 of them in second grade and one in third grade. Her classroom fostered student growth in compassion, empathy, resilience, citizenship, and growth mindset as well as academics through dynamic learning experiences and an intentional and creative approach to integrating SEL with curriculum.

As a teacher leader, Wendy has led change and growth focused on trauma-informed practices, SEL for students and adults, hands-on learning opportunities, environmental citizenship, and character-building programs. With others, she established several programs at her school, including "Girls on the Run" and a hands-on school garden program through a partnership with Healthy Foods for Healthy Kids. Working to positively impact the community around her, she also worked to establish a community recycling event with the Delaware Solid Waste Authority. Wendy enjoyed serving as a member of the Delaware SEL Core Team, as a Next Generation Science Standard teacher leader at the state level, and as the Teacher of the Year member on the Delaware State Board of Education. Wendy loves facilitating dynamic, engaging professional development sessions both locally and nationally and is known for her energy, passion, and effectiveness among participants and attendees.

Wendy is a leader and has been recognized with numerous awards over the course of her career. These include being named a Delaware Compassion Champion, an Outstanding Educator Award Winner by the Delaware STEM Council, an NEA Foundation Global Learning Fellow culminating with fieldwork in South Africa, and an NEA Foundation Excellence in Education Award Winner. Wendy also received a Presidential Award for Excellence in Teaching Science and has been named an Outstanding Environmental Educator and a Green Schools Changemaker. She enjoyed serving as an *Empatico* Empathy

Fellow and a *No Kid Hungry* School Breakfast Fellow. Wendy also spent a semester as a full-time faculty member at Delaware Technical Community College in the Bachelor of Science Education Program, where she enjoyed connecting with and teaching future educators.

As an expert practitioner, she regularly shares her expertise on SEL and learning in podcasts, blogs, and articles and on social media. She has partnered with the NEA, Savvas Learning, McGraw Hill, The Cult of Pedagogy Podcast, and was featured in an article on SEL in Time. Since 2019, she has facilitated professional development for Kristin Souers and Pete Hall, the authors of *Fostering Resilient Learners*, and continues her work through Wendy Turner Consulting offering professional development and coaching in SEL.

Wendy received her bachelor of science in accounting from Boston College and her master's degree in elementary education from Wilmington University after a successful career in accounting and finance with large companies for 17 years.

You can find Wendy hanging out with her husband Dan, her teenage kids Maggie and Mike, and her German shepherd Bella in suburban Wilmington, Delaware. In her spare time, she loves to spend time in nature, read, watch movies, eat great food, exercise, and travel. Find Wendy on social media on Twitter, Facebook, LinkedIn, Wakelet or contact her at wendy@wendyturner-consulting.com and www.wendyturnerconsulting.com.

Foreword

"I proudly proclaim myself a Warrior of SEL."

You're going to read that line in just a little bit, depending on the pace and intensity with which you read professional texts like this, and let me assure you of one thing: it's absolutely true.

The author of that statement and of this book, Wendy Turner, is the real deal. When it comes to the big-picture, real-life, purpose-driven, human-connection parts of education, Wendy just gets it.

She gets it. What else can I say? She understands it. And she's drawn to it, less like a moth to a flame because of the obvious result and more like a bird to the sky because of its natural, obvious, and fitting manner. She feels it, breathes it, learns it, absorbs it, revels in it, and in all other ways, lives it.

What's this mysterious "it" that I mention? Some, as Wendy does, refer to it as SEL: social emotional learning. Others may fancy "it" as EQ, or emotional intelligence. Maybe you've heard of terms like Culture of Safety, a nest, or a positive learning environment if you're engaged in schooling and have read one of the two books on childhood trauma I co-authored with Kristin Souers.

When I was a newer, fresher teacher, I knew that my focus had to be on the human beings sharing a space with me, the ones I was to educate and raise and protect and love and educate and nurture for 10-month spans. Curriculum is great and helpful and all, and lesson plans and teaching strategies are all well and good, and ... I learned the phrase "I teach kids, not content" early on. I was alerted to the importance of relationships by my mentors and then, more urgently, by my students. Human connection had to become a priority, but I didn't know exactly how to engage in that work most productively.

With a lot of my kids, I was able to tap into that *je ne sais quoi* that allowed me to build healthy, strong, positive relationships. Most of it happened rather naturally or at least subconsciously. We laughed together, talked about things we had in common. I attended their concerts and sporting events and bought way too many cookies from them for our school's fundraisers. I even went way out of my way to teach choir (something I had no history or skills to do), led a chess club (again, how does a knight move?), and pretended to be interested in a lot of things ... *because I was interested in the well-being of kids who were interested in a lot of things*. In retrospect, it all made sense. At the time, I'll be honest, I was winging it. It wasn't working for *all* of my students, and *all* is the only number that matters in education.

And guess what? Because my focus was so entirely and relentlessly focused on the kids under my care, I completely ignored a glaring truth: My own social and emotional well-being is a prerequisite to healthy relationship-building and happy, regulated, learning-ready students.

That's right, like Russian nesting dolls or an avalanche or the Fibonacci sequence, SEL builds upon itself and grows in its power and impact. I can be good to others only if I'm good to myself first. "You must learn to love yourself before you can love others," they say. This all sounds fine and dandy, but no one ever explicitly taught me how to do that, and no mentor or coursework or field guide ever explicitly mentioned "Adult SEL" and the importance of grown-ups tending to their own SEL skills, their emotional well-being, their mental fitness, their relationship with self, their ability to regulate, and their ability to moderate stress in order to maintain (or recover) the executive functions of the brain.

What Wendy has done here is extend the public conversation about what it means to be a human being when working with, raising, nurturing, coaching, educating, counseling, and otherwise supporting young people. It starts with the grown-ups and the specific skills and approaches essential to our Adult SEL.

She has laid out a suitable framework for how to do the work that many of us in education know in our bones we must do but lack the know-how and confidence to do effectively. She has provided solid definitions of terms that we use so ubiquitously they're in danger of losing all practical communicative value. And she's provided examples of strategy after strategy that we can employ in our daily work to attune to ourselves … in order to help raise and develop young people into the amazing not-so-young people they can most certainly become.

Throughout this book, you'll pick up on the very deliberate, strategic approaches that Wendy shares in order to support your practice, which will undoubtedly lead to a healthier, happier you. A you with deeper emotional wherewithal, more powerful collegial relationships, and a stronger sense of self awareness, problem-solving, and investment in connections.

What you will also pick up is the very deliberate, strategic utilization of Wendy's true, core self. Through her stories, anecdotes, reflections, and inner monologue, she'll reveal herself as an authentic, genuine human being. Like I said, she's the real deal.

This isn't the story of someone who leaves her 9-to-5 job, swoops into education and immediately has it all figured out, earns a Teacher of the Year award, and decides to write a book. Quite the contrary. This is the story of someone who leaves her 9-to-5 job, swoops into education, and finds it steeped with muck. As she plods along early in her journey, she questions her path, her destination, even her very essence. You'll accompany Wendy, warts and all, as she asks questions relentlessly, tries and struggles and tries again, and continues to modify and improve her own practice in order to better meet her students' (and our community's) needs.

Isn't that what education is all about? That's why I say Wendy just gets it. I know that SEL and similar terms rile some folks up, and that's typical of the unknown. We fear it, and our fear then closes our minds to the possibility of something healthy, something loving, something positive. Thank goodness for Wendy! She removes the mystery from SEL. She understands that the prioritization of Adult SEL will cascade throughout the entire school community. She opens the curtain to the tender underbelly of human connection in education. She clarifies the murk so those terms that some folks fear become real ideas – real, powerful, wholesome, noble, beneficial ideas. Ideas that can change the world.

For the past five years or so, Wendy has shared these real ideas, accompanied by real strategies, in schools, districts, and classrooms across the country. We met after Kristin Souers and I presented a workshop on childhood trauma to an audience of educators in Delaware, and Wendy introduced herself to us. Five minutes later, Kristin and I were convinced that Wendy's energy, integrity, track record, and passion for this topic would be a perfect complement to our work. I've marveled at her tenacity and ability to resonate with educators ever since – and, based on the feedback we've received from her workshops and keynotes, I'm not alone.

So dig into this book. Read and absorb the messages and the lessons for yourself, and as you do, I encourage you to engage in the reflective prompts Wendy provides so you can challenge yourself to question, to learn, to grow, to evolve, and to embrace a path that leads everywhere positive. Then, perhaps you, too, can proclaim yourself a Warrior of SEL.

Pete Hall
Coeur d'Alene, Idaho
May 24, 2023

Introduction

My Social Emotional Learning Journey

Growing up, I never wanted to be a teacher. Ever. The thought never crossed my mind. I don't come from a long line of educators, and we weren't friends with anyone who was a teacher. My mom stayed home with the kids, and my dad went off into a city each day to work in an office. I wanted to do the same thing as my dad. I wanted to be a business person, carry a briefcase, wear a suit, and commute into the city to work. So I majored in accounting in college and got a job after graduation in a big city where I could work in an office in a skyscraper and do a business job, specifically public accounting. I was proud and happy. But later, much later, I realized I wanted more. I was no longer fulfilled by my office job and responsibilities. At the same time, each of my sisters had a child, so I found myself around children more often at family gatherings and parties. I loved being around those kids! I was surprisingly able to connect with them. I derived joy from our interactions, and started to think maybe, just maybe, I could be a teacher. This was an important moment of self-awareness in my journey.

Fast forward to an unremarkable day when our daughter was 6 months old. I was sitting in my cubicle at work in my corporate job, and I just realized I didn't want to do it anymore and certainly could not for the next 20 years. I picked up the phone, called my husband, and asked him what he thought about me becoming a teacher. Long pause. Silence. I was getting worried about what he might say. But he didn't drop the phone or hang up and finally said, "Go for it, you'll be great". My husband Dan has always been my biggest fan, supporter, and cheerleader for my adventures in life. So, for the next four years, I worked full-time at my corporate job and attended school at night to earn a master's degree in elementary education. Looking back at that time, I realize it was one of the most challenging of my life. I would work all day and then attend class at least once a week from 5 to 9 p.m. I started in 2006, long before hybrid or asynchronous learning opportunities were available, so it was always in-person, away from home. I remember it was incredibly hard. I recall being at class one of the first times our daughter had a fever; she was home with a babysitter until my husband arrived home from work. I felt the mom guilt. I remember giving a presentation in class about a week before our son was born, being uncomfortable and very pregnant. But what I also remember is that it was one of the most exciting periods of my life. One might think that being married, living in the suburbs, and having kids could be the beginning of something monotonous, typical, and maybe boring, but this path took my life in a totally different direction, and it was amazing! I absolutely loved learning and enjoyed being back in a classroom. It was the beginning of the adoption of a true growth mindset for me and a turning point in my journey as a human being. I truly enjoyed my instructors, their tales from the front lines of education, my classmates, and moving along the continuum of preparation toward being an educator. I will forever cherish the opportunity and experience. A valuable lesson I learned is that we never stop growing and evolving. Become a teacher at 40? Heck yes! With the support of Dan, I never looked back and I went on to achieve my dream. Without really knowing it, I was living in and through a powerful social emotional learning (SEL) moment, bathed in self-awareness and a growth mindset.

When I think about why this happened and how I even had the mindset to do it, I think back to my parents. They came from incredibly different circumstances and situations in life, but both showed me, clearly, that we can do hard things as an adult and create new opportunities around our passions. Here are their stories.

My mother grew up in a very rural area, the first daughter of teenage parents who were together for a very short time. She did not come from much. At a young age, she knew she would have to work hard and dream big to leave her small town and attend college so she could live the life she envisioned. As a young girl, she boarded a plane to South America for an exchange program with her church. This extraordinary experience motivated her to do well and seek out big experiences. She put herself through community college and moved to New York City to be a merchandise buyer for a department store in her early 20s. When my parents divorced years later, she worked as a secretary to support us and then earned a degree in accounting attending college at night, her first four-year degree. Years later, she attended college at night once again to earn a degree in nursing in her 50s. In her 50s! What I did pales in comparison with her accomplishments. I am so grateful I had her example and support during this time I was earning my teaching degree and being a wife and a mom. Mom, I appreciate you so much. Thanks for being there for me and encouraging me to follow my dreams.

My father worked in accounting and finance jobs most of his life; that's where my initial inspiration came from. As my parents divorced, he left his corporate job and started his own business as a financial advisor to athletes. His love of sport intersected with his financial expertise, and he made it work. Some of his favorite clients were baseball player Yogi Berra, sportscaster Jim Nantz, basketball player Mark Eaton, and football player Tim Green. He went on to success and was able to earn enough to send his four children to college and fund retirement. At the time of his retirement, he sold his successful business and was able to say, "I did it!". His steadfastness, dedication, and perseverance are still an inspiration to me as I continue to evolve today. Thanks, Dad, for all of your love, support, and encouragement over the years and for your example.

An important moment in my journey was my graduation as an educator in 2010. After four years of school at night, I had finished my master's degree. Here are some pictures of that special day. Our son did not even exist at the onset of the journey! This day will forever live on in my soul as both an ending and a beginning. So many moments in our lives have elements of both intertwined within them. I was done being a student and would soon be a teacher.

Figure 0.1 My husband and I at my Elementary Education master's degree graduation ceremony in 2010.

Figure 0.2 My kids and I at my Elementary Education master's degree graduation ceremony in 2010.

Figure 0.3 Our silly kids at my Elementary Education master's degree graduation ceremony in 2010.

My journey as an educator has been punctuated with so many conflicting emotions: moments of joy, fear, power, helplessness, and hope as well as clarity and confusion. I'll share them throughout the book. One of the most powerful moments came unexpectedly in the first two weeks of my teaching career, when a student in my class lost a family member. I was paralyzed with fear about the situation. I quite simply did not know what to do. So I thought. I cried. And I reached out for help. Counselors, administrators, and peers helped me to navigate the moment for myself and my class. The biggest takeaway I had from the situation was that we need to go *through* big emotions, not around them. We can't pretend things aren't happening; we have to face them, head on. We have to be human and vulnerable and real if we are going to get through life. We need to understand and use empathy. It's messy but necessary. This became part of my core beliefs as an educator, and I have embraced and worked to live that ever since. Again, I was living through a significant SEL moment; this time, the moment had tentacles that stretched into and through self-awareness, self-management, social awareness, relationship skills, and responsible decision-making – all five core SEL skills.

Although I didn't realize it at the time, I was thinking and talking about and living in SEL, what I call the fine art of being human. This idea has always been part of my core beliefs. In an early, clumsy version of my teaching philosophy penned during my years in night school, I said something like "I need to teach my students how to be successful humans". I knew this was central to the learning we needed to do, but I did not yet know exactly what that meant or what it looked like. Every day, with every small experience, I learned more and more about what it looks like, feels like, sounds like, and how it exists in a classroom and a school. As my skills as an educator evolved in SEL, so have my personal SEL skills as a human being. We can't separate that growth. It comes to us as whole humans, not just personally or professionally.

After six years in the classroom, I was honored to be named the 2017 Delaware Teacher of the Year. A year of extraordinary experiences, opportunities, and connections with amazing individuals from around the country, and the world, was born.

Figure 0.4 I am the 2017 Delaware Teacher of the Year.

Figure 0.5 Addressing the Delaware Legislature in 2017.

This is not an award for being the best teacher. Rather, it is a recognition of someone who can be recognized as a model for the education profession and creates a positive and inspiring impact. There are countless teachers among us who do just that, each and every day. I believe part of the reason I received this honor was my work in SEL. As a result of this incredible honor and opportunity, I was able to connect with fantastic educators around the country and best-selling authors and to share my story with many different audiences. I advocated for trauma-informed support for students just as there was a significant investment in this work at many levels in my home state of Delaware. I was fortunate that my chosen platform was one that many individuals in many different systems were talking about and focusing on during my year of service as the teacher of the year.

At the same time, I started to learn more about SEL for students and adults. I was able to be a part of growth and change through book studies, professional development, and training where I was able to take a leadership role at various times. I will forever treasure this time in my life. It was an explosion of growth for me. This allowed me to be brave and innovative in my classroom and in my own way take some of the ideas and concepts I was learning about and bring them alive with my students and the adults I worked with. Was it an SEL moment, or really, a period of powerful social-emotional growth again? Yes! Most definitely.

I became known as a warrior of SEL. I connected with educators around the world through social media and was able to activate and develop my teacher voice by writing blogs and articles and appearing on podcasts to share my strategies and insights around SEL. I developed expert-level knowledge of SEL with the help of research and the knowledge and expertise and support of state leaders. This growth in knowledge and my personal SEL skill development served me well through the Covid-19 pandemic. I was a teacher, like so many of you, on March 13, 2020, when everything changed. Forever. One of the most powerful of these projects was an interview I recorded in April 2020 for The Cult of Pedagogy Podcast called "Social Emotional Learning: Not Just For Kids". The podcast explains my approach of living SEL skills myself and modeling them in the classroom.

I am a practitioner, not a researcher. My lab is my classroom and my life. I am also a regular person who wants to create a positive impact around me. I want to do it with joy, kindness, optimism, and positivity. I work in my space and within my sphere of influence to learn and grow and share with others tools and resources to help people go forward in the name of SEL in a successful way. Busy educators need specific, actionable, and concrete steps to build their own SEL practice and grow their confidence with an action plan. Lots of teachers know that practicing mindfulness and kindness and making good choices have to do with SEL. But many do not know what SEL actually is or how exactly to explain it succinctly to others or how to engage in it with their students. That's where I come in. My goal is to provide all of you with an understanding of exactly what SEL is as well as a series of specific and actionable ideas and ways to practice your own SEL skills, build habits, and then create SEL success in your classrooms with students of all ages and adults in our school communities. Keep your pen, phone, and laptop handy while you read. As a tool, this book includes space for reflecting at the end of each chapter as well as QR codes and links to take you right to the resources I have found to be helpful.

In my opinion, SEL is the foundation of the schoolhouse, the ground floor of learning, and, without it, the institution will crumble. SEL is critically important today. We know this. Especially in light of the impacts of Covid-19 on students and educators, it's more important than ever. Many people know and understand its importance in education today but struggle with how to implement it successfully in the classroom. Some people may think SEL is for little kids on a carpet and doesn't have a place or time in content-specific courses. Some may think working on SEL skills is not their job; it's for counselors to do or meant for an advisory period. I disagree! Living and teaching SEL are all of our jobs! But this is a challenge. Educators are overwhelmed with all they have on their plates and are facing significant burnout, and they may think they just can't do it; they might feel like they can't add one more thing to their day. All of these thoughts around SEL are completely valid. That's why I'm committed to creating a resource to meet this challenge and support my fellow educators.

I'm writing this book because I want to solve a problem. The challenge I see as I train, talk to, and work with educators around the country is that not everyone in education knows enough about SEL. Many teacher preparation programs do not include specific instruction in SEL or how to integrate it with academics, so there's a knowledge gap when educators enter our workforce. Then, SEL training and skills become another thing to have to work on, nurture, and grow on an educator's already overflowing plate. I want to create a resource for educators that immediately helps with this problem and knowledge gap. This book will help you determine where you are with respect to SEL, pique your curiosity, and help you get started with building your confidence and competence around SEL.

My goal is to foster curiosity, confidence, and competence in SEL. I want to help adults grow their skills and foster skill development with staff and with students of all ages. In this book, I'll share tools to help you understand SEL, grow your own skills, and weave them successfully into your school and classroom culture and education setting. I embrace research and well-known frameworks in my own way and offer a concrete path for you to start your journey. Think about an SEL highway. It has an on-ramp and multiple lanes on which to travel. I'll show you how to figure out where you are and then travel on the road to SEL success.

Embracing Adult SEL is for all of us. This is a resource for educators looking to increase their knowledge and tools in the classroom as well as any other learning space in the schoolhouse, including the counselor's office, the conference room, the hallway, wherever we find ourselves. We can bring SEL alive for ourselves and our community. It's for leaders who want to inspire and connect with their teams so they can work better together and do more in the name of better outcomes for themselves and their students. It's for families and caregivers who want to bring ideas around SEL home so they can create safe and supportive spaces for each other while we live through the impact of a global pandemic. Finally, it's for any human being who is interested in a story of growth, learning, and impact and would like some inspiration while they learn concrete strategies to help them become more successful human beings. It can be read over the weekend so you can try some of the strategies on Monday morning. It's for new teachers and veterans. It's for all of us.

Here you can see a more recent picture of me and my family. The change you see here represents the journey I have taken, the changes I have experienced, and the growth in my life. This book is so special to me because it is the manifesto of my experiences and the change and growth I have experienced as a human being, an educator, and simply a person who wants to learn and share with others.

Figure 0.6 Family vacation, 2022.

SEL matters for all of us. It matters more for us educators than for people in other professions because we are in the business of raising up human beings. When we better understand, live, and model effective SEL skills and competencies, we can help them come alive for our students, which will increase student success in school and life.

This work is about my story as a human being as much as it is about SEL. That's because I can't separate my identity as a human being from my role as an educator or a mom and wife. I would never have gained as much personal or professional success without doing this SEL work. My growth and work in this area have benefited me as an educator and as a human being. I live in SEL every day. I have become a better wife, mom, and friend in this work. I am so grateful you have chosen to pick up this book and start your SEL journey with me. We all need a roadmap to move forward. Additionally, please note this roadmap is judgment-free! Something my experience has taught me is that we are all very much our own human beings with a unique and complex set of experiences, preferences, beliefs, and styles of learning and doing things. As with my students, I try to present multiple ways to access content and knowledge and empower people to embrace it and show their learning in multiple ways. The same goes for Adult SEL. This book is a collection of options, an SEL menu for all of you to digest and use in the most suitable way for your success. Keep your phone and laptop handy while you read. I've included links and QR codes for the resources I share, so you can check out videos, articles, blogs, and websites as you go. I've also included space for you to jot notes in reflection at the end of each chapter and have added a link to an online reflection tool. Please process information and ideas in the way that makes the most sense for you. If you are able to walk away from this book with even one or two new strategies to try to build your Adult SEL skills, I'll be thrilled. The road stretches out long in front of us. I wish you safe and happy travels on your journey to SEL success!

1

Understanding SEL

Where Are You on the Road to SEL Success?

What if someone told you that there was something you could do in your classroom that would boost academic achievement by over 10%? This same thing also helps kids develop social skills which will help them to be more successful in school and in life. Would you do it? I bet you would at least want to know what it is, how it works and how to do it. You would probably want to try it. That something is social emotional learning or SEL.

Teaching is hard. Incredibly hard. Looking back, I don't think I had any idea about the complexity and nuances of teaching when I called my husband that day from my cubicle. We have to make hundreds of important decisions multiple times per day. Creating a safe and supportive learning environment for anywhere from 20 to 150 students, depending on what you teach, is the norm. We have to manage expectations, emotions, and conditions we can't control. Our work environment is constantly changing. Strong organization skills as well as communication skills are as important as a strong pedagogy. It's a lot! Knowing about and trying out different practices and strategies can help us help ourselves as well as our students. SEL is one of these practices.

SEL is critically important, especially today, perhaps now more than ever given the impacts of the Covid-19 pandemic on educators and students. Students have fewer social and academic skills than they normally would. Educators, leaders, and students of all ages have higher levels of worry, anxiety, and fear. Everyone in the education community has been pushed to the brink to be innovative and compassionate and show grit and perseverance in solving problems and getting their jobs done. Teacher burnout is a real issue, and people are leaving the profession in a way not seen before. Embracing the skills and competencies that are part of SEL can help both adults and students be more successful in the classroom and handle the work before them. But there are a few challenges that arise with this work.

The Challenges

Not everyone has the same amount of curiosity, confidence, and competence with SEL. This creates the complex problem of how to train educators uniformly and effectively in what SEL is and how to do it. The root cause of this challenge lies in the fact that not everyone receives training and coursework in SEL in pre-service education programs. I know this through my work as a professional development facilitator. I always ask the educators I work with if they ever learned about SEL in their preparation program. Few hands go up and this is universal in my experience working with educators around the country. Many educator preparation programs include a class called "Classroom Management," which focuses on how to run the classroom. Given my reputation as an expert practitioner in the area of SEL, I have repeatedly been asked to guest lecture in college classes on the topic of SEL because it is not a formal part of coursework. For me, SEL is a huge component of creating a safe and supportive culture, in effect "running the classroom" and creating culture and engagement. I would love to reimagine a course called "Classroom Management" as "Building Classroom Culture and Student Engagement". SEL is a key component of this work along with trauma-invested practices as well as culturally responsive teaching. Elements of SEL connect with important elements of these practices as well.

Many schools and districts have adopted SEL curricula and dedicated time to SEL. This is wonderful! However, it doesn't mean that the adults using the curriculum are adequately knowledgeable about why SEL is so important, what the research says, or even how to implement the lessons and curriculum well. Integrating SEL with academics is another skill to learn. It's an essential component of this work and a necessary ingredient to doing it well.

My mission is to foster curiosity, confidence, and competence with respect to SEL. I believe educators will enjoy more job satisfaction if they grow their own SEL skills and embed them into their classrooms, both through modeling and integration with academic instruction. There is a pathway to this and it begins with one's self and embracing Adult SEL. An important question to ask yourself is "Where am I with respect to social emotional learning?"

Where Are You with SEL?

During Covid-19, a simple but powerful graphic circulated on social media laying out different zones of awareness for individuals to understand where they were with respect to Covid-19. I also saw it being used for understanding in the journey of anti-racism. I saw the graphic on Twitter and know it was also shared on LinkedIn. This graphic was incredibly helpful to me and helped me to create a path to move forward, in growth, around both ideas. It outlined a fear zone, a learning zone, and a growth zone. I am going to use a similar graphic to explain how to find out where we are and move forward in learning about SEL. The original graphic looked similar to this one.

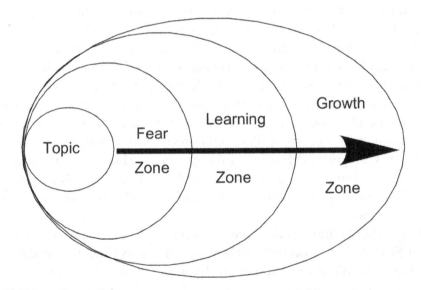

Figure 1.1 Zones of SEL.

Which Zone Are You In?

I'm going to adapt this model for understanding with respect to SEL. I'll share what it means to be in the Fear Zone, the Curiosity Zone, the Confidence Zone, and the Competence Zone.

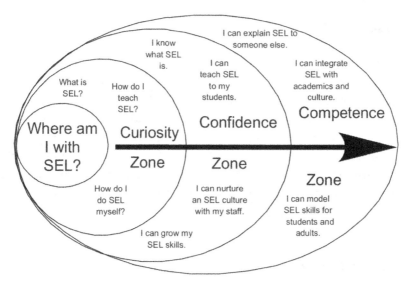

Figure 1.2 Where am I with SEL?

The Fear Zone

This place is not even visible in the model. In this zone, we hide. In the SEL Fear Zone, one doesn't know anything about SEL and doesn't want to learn anything about it. Research tells us that the positive impacts are numerous and far-reaching, but in this zone, research is ignored and learning and growth do not take place. It is a valley of stagnation, an empty harbor, and a place of still silence. Someone in this zone may say things like "I don't care about SEL", "SEL is not my job", "I don't have time for this", or even "SEL is harmful". The Fear Zone is outside any of the circles in the graphic. It is an empty place without ideas or an entry point to learning about and growing in SEL. This is also a place of a fixed mindset around SEL. SEL does not live or grow here.

The Curiosity Zone

In this zone, we learn. In the SEL Curiosity Zone, we ask questions! We are open to learning, and we start to take knowledge and understanding about SEL into our hearts and mind. This is a part of a growth mindset, asking questions and believing we can learn. In this zone, we can ask "What is SEL?", "How can I teach SEL?", and "How do I engage in SEL myself?" as well as "How can I model 'SEL' for my students and peers as part of my practice?" We grow in the Curiosity Zone.

The Confidence Zone

In this zone, we practice. Here is where we not only grow, we gain confidence! Once we reach a place of curiosity and learn facts and knowledge about SEL, we can grow our SEL muscles and bring SEL skills and competencies to life, in both our personal and professional lives. We move from questions to statements. Statements one may make in this zone are "I know what SEL is", "I can teach SEL to my students", and "I can grow my own SEL skills". With knowledge, understanding, and practice, our SEL muscles grow stronger and we can see and feel progress on a daily basis. We start to use SEL skills more often and learn to use them well.

The Competence Zone

In this zone, we thrive! We enjoy living in SEL and our growth mindset and we can see the results. SEL is a central part of our personal and professional life. In this zone, we can confidently make statements such as "I can explain SEL to someone else", "I can seamlessly incorporate SEL into academic learning", and "I can model SEL skills for students and adults as part of my daily habits". We know when we are having an SEL moment, what competency it relates to, and how to use our skills for better outcomes. Here, we live in SEL and we help others grow their skills as well.

In *The Light We Carry*, Michelle Obama perfectly describes the Competence Zone, sharing "And competence, I've learned, is what sits on the flip side of fear" (Obama, 2022, p. 66). "My parents nudged my brother and me forward into competence, creating opportunities for us to feel a sense of certainty and mastery each time we conquered something new" (Obama, 2022, p. 67). The ideas and strategies here can help anyone move forward in their understanding and practice of SEL in an understandable, accessible, and organized way, moving toward competence.

If we think of SEL as a highway, a means to travel efficiently and well, these zones help us determine where we are. The Fear Zone is back roads, they are slow-moving and twisty, and we can easily get lost trying to get somewhere. The Curiosity Zone is the on-ramp to and the righthand lane of the highway; it is an entry point, a direct conduit to the place of traveling quickly and efficiently to where we are going. It is safe and moves at a pace that bathes us in comfort as we learn. It is always open and it allows us to get off, rest, and process, as needed. This is where we access "rest stops" on the road, pause, and rejuvenate as needed. The Confidence Zone is the middle lane of a three-lane highway. Here, we have access to curiosity as well as competence through practice. As we learn, or drive, down the SEL superhighway, we can move from the Curiosity Zone to the Confidence Zone in steps as we learn. We can change lanes as we practice and build our skills. The Competence Zone is the fast lane; it is where we can travel and move quickly and efficiently, wrapped in the strength of our SEL skills as we bring them to our students and staff and continue to grow them personally in our daily lives. Of course, we can continue to learn and grow as we change lanes and rest as needed. Here, we can move right into the fast lane often, without problems and with a feeling of comfort.

Let's look at some of the questions in the various zones.

What is SEL?

Before we look at the formal definition of SEL according to a leading organization, I want to explore the three words that make it up with the Merriam-Webster online dictionary.

TABLE 1.1 Definitions of social, emotional, and learning

Social	*Marked by or passed in pleasant **companionship** with friends or associates*
Emotional	*Markedly aroused or agitated in **feeling** or sensibilities*
Learning	*The **understanding** and **information** gained from being educated*

So if we try to put all of this together, we can understand that SEL may mean something like "understanding and information around feelings and sensibilities derived by pleasant companionship with others".

In December 2022, Education Week assistant editor Arianna Prothero asked experts what SEL means in her outstanding article "What Does SEL Mean Anyway? 7 Experts Break It Down". The responses, while all different, get at the same big idea, the idea of being a successful human being with explicit skill development. I love the depth and breadth of these responses and all they encompass. Key words and ideas are highlighted in these quotes.

> "Social emotional learning is the **process** by which children and adults learn how to solve **inter- and intrapersonal problems** in order to maximize their ability to flourish across environments."
> —*David Adams, CEO, The Urban Assembly*

"Social and emotional learning is the reason my son loves school again and can focus on learning. It is the **relationship** that he has built with a supportive teacher and the way he has developed **skills** to process his **emotions**, make friends, practice curiosity, and **solve problems**."

—*Aaliyah A. Samuel, president and CEO, Collaborative for Academic, Social, and Emotional Learning, or CASEL*

"SEL can't be addressed only in a 10-minute morning meeting or every Thursday, fourth period. It can't be isolated in occasional assemblies for students or in workshops for teachers. SEL—which includes the **principles, tools, and strategies** that build self- and social awareness, healthy emotion regulation, and responsible decision making—has to be an everyday thing and **part of the school's DNA**. There needs to be a common language among all stakeholders. It has to be **integrated** into leadership, instruction, faculty meetings, family engagement, hiring procedures, and policies."

—*Marc Brackett, professor, Yale School of Medicine, and Director of the YaleCenter for Emotional Intelligence*

"When I use a metaphor to teach SEL, I use fire fighting versus fire prevention. If I'm a forest ranger, and there are constantly forest fires, yes, I'm going to go put out those fires. But it makes a lot more sense for me to teach everyone at the campsite fire prevention. If I can **teach people** how to manage their **emotions, resolve conflicts, and bounce back from setbacks**, I'm going to put out less fires. ... What we need to do is teach, proactively, **skills** that help kids do fire prevention. Like, how to access mental health resources, how to bounce back from setbacks, how to build healthy **relationships**."

—*R. Keeth Matheny, former teacher, founder of SEL Launchpad*

"Brick-masonry structures are made with bricks bonded together with mortar these structures can withstand even the most powerful storms. SEL is like the mortar. It **connects** people together by teaching how to develop and maintain **relationships** even when we disagree or are different from one another. SEL is like the mortar. It connects practices, **skills**, and **emotions** to help us create a healthy identity. SEL is like the mortar. It connects individual bricks of knowledge helping us to effectively apply ourselves and achieve goals. SEL is like the mortar. **It creates empathetic, contributing, resilient humans who can withstand even the most powerful storms.**"

—*Trish Shaffer, MTSS/SEL coordinator, Washoe County School District*

> "When you think about setting up a fish tank, you go in and purchase your fish, gravel, filter, little plants, all of that. When you are creating learning environments, you have the curriculum, the Texas essential knowledge and skills, lessons of how students will get an understanding of all these concepts. And you have the water. But if your pH is off, your fish will not survive. **You can have great facilities, content, people, but if people don't feel like they belong, unsafe, disconnected, or unable to regulate their emotions, learning will not take place."**
> —Statia Paschel, director of SEL and Cultural Proficiency and Inclusiveness, Austin Independent School District

You can read the full article here.

TABLE 1.2 Link and QR code for "What Does SEL Mean Anyway? 7 Experts Break It Down"

Resource	Link to Access	QR Code to Access
Article: "What Does SEL Mean Anyway? 7 Experts Break It Down"	https://bit.ly/EASELedw	

I believe SEL is the base layer of learning. It's the foundation of the schoolhouse and the heartbeat of education. Without it, the institution crumbles. When asked about this by a national reporter for *TIME* magazine, I explained: "It's really all about helping kids develop and nurture skills that help them be successful human beings - which is going to translate into success in school, and then outside of school, on the sports field, on the bus, in their homes, in the community, as they grow into adults in society." Like all of the experts above, I believe SEL is a critical element of school culture and learning and a key success factor for students and adults. It can't be isolated in stand-alone lessons. Skills do have to be taught explicitly but then must be interwoven into the fabric of learning. I would never be able to teach without it. It's critical for my students' overall success. I know I need to have a strong command of what SEL means and be able to embrace learning and skill growth in each of the five competencies myself in order to help them come alive for my students. SEL is absolutely essential in my classroom.

People in the education world know I am passionate and knowledgeable about SEL. The Social Institute, a company that provides a gamified, online learning platform that empowers students to navigate their social world through SEL, social media, and technology to fuel their health, happiness, and future success, quoted me on Twitter in August 2021.

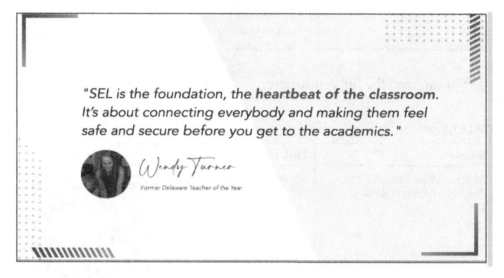

Figure 1.3 The Social Institute tweeted this image on August 18, 2021, shared with permission.

You can access a blog I wrote for The Social Institute on teaching SEL during Covid here.

TABLE 1.3 Link and QR code for "Teaching SEL During Covid: Lessons Learned and Three Tips for Educators Moving Forward"

Resource	Link to Access	QR Code to Access
Blog: *"Teaching SEL During Covid: Lessons Learned and Three Tips for Educators Moving Forward"*	https://bit.ly/EASELsi	

The Casel Social Emotional Learning Model

CASEL, a champion of SEL since 1994, defines SEL as

> "a process that helps children and adults acquire and apply the knowledge, skills, and attitudes to develop healthy identities, manage emotions and achieve personal and collective goals, in addition to showing empathy for others, maintaining supportive relationships and making responsible decisions."

Their competency model includes five core skills: self-awareness, self-management, social awareness, relationship skills, and responsible relationships. An important part of their framework is understanding that these skills are taught and practiced in classrooms and schools as well as in the community and that community stakeholders such as parents and families are an important part of SEL. In effect, we are all in this together. This multi-layered definition of SEL illustrates the depth and complexity of the topic. Each core skill has specific elements of focus; they are all interconnected and build on one another yet can be developed separately with very intentional practice. I agree they are all necessary for developing as a whole person, whether one is an adult or a child of any age. Specifically, I use Casel's definition of SEL as five core skills to augment my ideas around SEL being the base layer of education.

What Does the Research Say?

Research tells us that the benefits of SEL are positive. Through hundreds of studies, Casel has learned that "when students have supportive relationships and opportunities to develop and practice social, emotional, and cognitive skills across many different contexts, academic learning accelerates". Academic performance has been shown to increase by over 10%, and classroom behavior improves as well as student ability to manage stress and construct better attitudes about school, peers, and themselves. This is a compelling case to engage in SEL in districts, schools, and classrooms.

In a 2021 research survey by Learning Heroes and EDGE Research of over 1,400 diverse elementary and secondary parents, parents said that safety, academics, and social emotional needs are their top priorities; 58% of parents cited "Development of the whole child" as a top priority; 54% of those surveyed said it was important for students to develop life skills. Over 40% of families reported that they wanted students to develop social and emotional skills and caring, consistent, and supportive relationships with adults.

It's clear that interest in SEL skills and outcomes is very high in our post-Covid education and learning environment. States, districts, schools, and families want to help students grow skills to help them handle their myriad emotions, connect with each other and their communities, and make successful decisions. If this is the "what" is needed right now, then SEL is the "how".

Casel also evaluates SEL curriculum and programming in their incredibly useful program guide. Curriculum is part of SEL culture and is a very necessary component of SEL implementation. There is also a personal component that can be developed by classroom practitioners and school leaders independently. Individuals can benefit from having their own personal roadmap to SEL success that complements explicit SEL programming and other student supports. This will help grow their confidence and add to the everyday enjoyment of their job, creating a positive impact for both students and adults. My goal is to provide such a roadmap.

I am not a researcher but rather a practitioner. I have expert-level knowledge of SEL and 12 years of experience with SEL in the classroom, including successful implementation with academics. I have successfully facilitated professional learning around SEL for adults in all levels of education for over five years. My years of classroom experience have taught me there is no boundary to being creative and innovative with approaches to SEL understanding and implementation. My experience has also taught me to listen to kids, slow down, persevere, and share with my peers. I am excited to explain my ideas, strategies, and craft here. But first, how do we create the conditions for success on this road? We need understanding.

Understand SEL Deeply and Completely

If we are to be successful in developing our own Adult SEL and helping students foster their own skills, we must understand SEL deeply and completely in no uncertain terms. Before I mastered understanding of SEL with the five-part competency model, I had trouble explaining exactly what it was. Like so many others, I knew that ideas like kindness, gratitude, emotions, staying calm, and getting along with people were part of the big picture, but I didn't know how to succinctly explain SEL.

There are many wonderful and powerful views of SEL that are related to Casel's core skills and competency model. They can focus on mindsets, social standards, or character development. They all support students' growth as successful human beings. Your school or district may have already selected one for your students and could be in an implementation phase. That is great!

But there is still work that can be done by all of us personally to augment these structures and help us learn and grow in front of our community, whether it be educators or students. If I had relied on a formal curriculum only, I would never have developed my skills, awareness, and impact to the degree that I have been able to. This book contains many of the creative ideas I have tried and small and big moves that have allowed me to hone my expertise and grow into an accomplished SEL practitioner with expert-level knowledge and skills.

Supporting Social and Emotional Learning

The Learning Policy Institute (LPI) published a case study of San Jose University and Lakewood Elementary School on "Preparing Teachers to Support Social and Emotional Learning" by Hanna Melnick and Lorea Martinez. In it, they brilliantly lay out implications for Pre-service Teacher Education Programs, Implications for Schools, and Implications for Policy based on their work. I'll focus on "Implications for School" here, but I highly recommend reading the full case study to learn more. As someone who has taught and worked with pre-service educators as well as served as the Teacher Leader on the State Board of Education, the entire case study speaks to me in a deep and visceral way about where we can go to help with this work and make it more accessible and successful for everyone involved, particularly with respect to policy. You can access the full case study here.

TABLE 1.4 Link and QR code for "Preparing Teachers to Support Social and Emotional Learning"

Resource	Link to Access	QR Code to Access
Learning Policy Institute: *"Preparing Teachers to Support Social and Emotional Learning"*	https://bit.ly/EASELlpi	

A lack of SEL focus in most teacher prep programs creates a significant challenge in education. Many new teachers are often not adequately prepared to bring the power of SEL into their classrooms, and it becomes "one more thing" on the already overcrowded educator plate of duties and responsibilities. Districts and schools are then faced with the task of addressing these challenges in an efficient, organized, and uniform manner.

Regarding "Implications for School", LPI lays out several powerful lessons we can take from their work and understand how schools can effectively support SEL. These ideas can combat the challenges of SEL not being uniformly incorporated into teacher preparation. Here is my take on each of the ideas in the case study.

SEL must permeate the school. Everyone in the school needs to understand what SEL is and its importance in the education of the whole child. This includes educators, administrators, support staff, and other critical members of the schoolhouse. Often overlooked, nutrition staff, transportation staff, and members of the facilities team spend lots of time with students. They need to be included in the community of adult learners on SEL. Everyone needs an understanding of SEL and can learn how to grow their own skills and competencies. Additionally, the adult mindset must be open and accepting of the importance of SEL and understand it as a system, not a series of one-and-done lessons that can be checked off and completed in isolation.

Adult SEL matters. It's all about Adult SEL. Emotions are everywhere in education, with educators, leaders, and students. In the wake of the Covid-19 pandemic, emotions are bigger than ever, and we all need to work on how to manage them successfully. Regulated brains are teaching and learning brains. Adults can model effective emotional management and teach strategies for regulation. In my *Cult of Pedagogy* podcast called "Social Emotional Learning: Not Just For Kids", I explore specific strategies for this and will explain them in the coming chapters. You can access the podcast with the information in Table 1.5.

TABLE 1.5 Link and QR code for "Social Emotional Learning: Not Just For Kids"

Resource	Link to Access	QR Code to Access
Cult of Pedagogy Podcast: *"Social Emotional Learning: Not Just For Kids"*	https://bit.ly/EASELcultofped	

Teachers need to be part of the process. In education, we tend to do a woefully inadequate job of activating and supporting teacher agency with regard to learning and professional development. Professional development and training topics are often decided for teachers by others in the system, whether or not educators perceive them as valuable or not. Since educators are a critical piece of any SEL system, they are vital to its success. Leaders can increase buy-in and engagement by asking teachers what they know and how they would like to learn about SEL and by providing a wide variety of models to choose. These include acquiring knowledge in a group or individually, observations, role play, and independent practice with a coaching and feedback system. The possibilities for adult learning are endless, and educators will be able to come up with creative and powerful ideas for this learning when asked. Teacher leaders who have successful practices and expert-level knowledge can authentically relate the work to their peers.

High-quality, varied, and ongoing professional development is needed. SEL is a critical factor in school and student success, so we can't limit it to a one-and-done learning model. Schools and districts will benefit from creating a sustained learning and implementation plan that covers an entire school year and a sequence over several years at the system level. Educators are hungry for tools to help them implement SEL and feel good about it. A barrier to successful classroom implementation includes feelings of being overwhelmed and uncertainty about how to do it. Repeated practice, coaching, and feedback are required for mastery. Ongoing and meaningful professional development supports both the Confidence and Competence zones.

SEL assessment. There is so much value in data. We know this in education. Data helps us determine where we are so we can chart a path forward. Without it, we can drift. Data around SEL is tricky because it can be an area that is not formally assessed. However, data can be used to guide and inform classroom approaches and uncover trends. Gathering data here is critically important. This can be at the classroom, grade, school, or district level. It is valuable if it's gathered for both students and adults. Data can be simple or complex, and anonymous data reveals the current state. Data over time can identify growth or regression in specific areas. When we gather data around SEL, we are making a significant investment in the work.

Personal Implications

When we focus on SEL, we focus on the entire human. Educators who engage in SEL development will bring that curiosity, confidence, and competence to their personal lives with favorable results. When I started doing this work with great intention five years ago, I was far less skilled in all five of the competencies that are part of the Casel framework. I have now experienced explosive growth in all five core skill areas. I am more skilled at meeting challenges, navigating problems, connecting with others, and bouncing back from setbacks. I continue learning and moving forward. This work has allowed me to become a more effective and empathetic human being in all of my contexts: as a wife and mom, educator, friend, and a member of my extended family as well as the various communities I live in. Covid-19 intensified my need for learning and growth in certain areas, but I noticed and embraced the opportunities that presented themselves to me. And I am so glad I did!

Professional Implications

I proudly proclaim myself a Warrior of SEL. I have that reputation in education and regularly share my ideas and strategies with other educators. This practice has brought me a great deal of joy and has affirmed my practices. My friend, Dr. Melissa Collins, an award-winning, exceptional, and inspirational second-grade teacher in Memphis, Tennessee, writes this about me in her book *Your Teacher Leadership Journey*, Chapter 3: Teacher Sightings.

> "Meet Wendy Turner: Wendy is known to me as 'The Social Emotional Teacher'. Here is why: At the National Network of State Teacher of the Year [NNSTOY] conference… I spotted Wendy Turner during her TED (inspired) Talk. She was speaking [about] how she addressed SEL. She created an environment where students could articulate their emotions in her class. Wendy believes that SEL is "the foundation of learning, the ground floor of the building, and the foundation of the schoolhouse. Without it, the institution crumbles". Her TED (inspired) Talk was so compelling that I started following her on Twitter and Facebook. Wendy motivated and inspired me to expose my students to more social and emotional learning opportunities. I have a banner displayed in my room that asks "How are you feeling today?" Now my students place [identify] their emotions (e.g., happy, OK, sad, or mad). Wendy and I stay in contact through social media outlets. We also had an opportunity to travel to South Africa together as Global Fellows with the National Education Foundation. While on this trip I learned more about Wendy's passion for teaching and learning.
> (Collins, 2022, pp. 31–32)

I recently had an invitation from Melissa to be part of a webinar on SEL with the National Board. It was an incredibly fulfilling and growing experience! Every time I share in this work, I grow and learn myself. I'm so grateful for

Melissa's friendship and her inspiration. I'll share more about my story and best practices throughout this book. I'll also dive into each competency area in detail, providing actionable strategies you can use for growth and development in SEL, right away, no matter what zone you are in.

It's time to determine where you are with respect to SEL. Find out what SEL zone you are in and act on it. Using the visual below, ask yourself each of the questions in the Curiosity Zone. If you can't answer them succinctly and thoroughly, that's the zone you are in. If you can answer those questions, then move to the Confidence Zone. If the statements in this zone are true for you, then move to the Competence Zone. Even when we live in the Competence Zone, we can add to our tools and strategies and continue to grow in SEL. As I live, breathe, and work in the Competence Zone, I continually evolve as I learn and grow in this work. Wherever you are, that's great; that's where you are supposed to be. If we don't know where we are, we can't move forward. But know that you can move forward in SEL with a plan.

Given the importance of SEL, particularly in the wake of the Covid-19 pandemic, it is our responsibility to learn as much as we can about SEL and then practice and gain competence in modeling strong SEL skills and integrating them in our classrooms and learning spaces. With the privilege, power, and opportunity that come with being an educator, it's also our responsibility to do this. The research tells us that students will achieve greater outcomes and we'll also be more successful in our personal lives.

Additional Resources to Grow Your Understanding of SEL

To increase your understanding of SEL, consider spending time going through these resources. Everything I am sharing here has been very important in growing my understanding of SEL over the years.

Read "Why Every School Must Have a Social Emotional Learning Plan Prior to Reopening" by Dr. Byron McClure. In this article, Dr. McClure skillfully explains why SEL is so important today and weaves in personal experiences as well as research and information on trauma to explain the what and the why of SEL, especially in the context of Covid-19. I read this article and was stopped cold in my tracks by its power. I always pay attention when this happens to me, whether for a good or bad reason. I then shared the article on my Teacher of the Year Facebook page and saw it receive more attention and engagement than anything else I had ever posted. Ever. It is so powerful! I depend on this article often. I go back to it, I refer others to it, and it remains one of my favorite cherished resources. This article should help you understand what SEL is and why it's so important.

TABLE 1.6 Link and QR code for "Why Every School Must Have a Social Emotional Learning Plan Prior to Reopening"

Resource	Bitly Link to Access	QR Code to Access
Article: "*Why Every School Must Have a Social Emotional Learning Plan Prior to Reopening*"	https://bit.ly/EASELwhy	

I also recommend you take in this fantastic piece, another by Dr. McClure, "Did You Know that SEL Emerged Because of a Black Man? The True History of SEL". Again, I was captivated by the history and knowledge in this piece, and it immediately helped me deepen my understanding of SEL and its roots. This article also provides understanding in the "Curiosity Zone".

TABLE 1.7 Link and QR code for "Did You Know that SEL Emerged Because of a Black Man? The True History of SEL"

Resource	Bitly Link to Access	QR Code to Access
Article: "*Did You Know that SEL Emerged Because of a Black Man? The True History of SEL*"	https://bit.ly/EASELdid	

Check out the "Lessons for SEL" YouTube channel. "Lessons for SEL" was founded by Dr. McClure, the author of the articles I recommend above in the "Curiosity Zone". Here, you'll see lessons on SEL you can implement in the classroom very easily. You'll start to have an idea of what SEL instruction looks and sounds like in an accessible format of quick video lessons and group reflection prompts. I used lots of resources for direct instruction of SEL skills which is a necessary part of bringing SEL alive in the classroom. You can try some of this yourself and take note of your own thoughts, feelings, questions, successes, and challenges around bringing SEL into the classroom.

TABLE 1.8 Link and QR code for the "Lessons for SEL" YouTube Channel

Resource	Bitly Link to Access	QR Code to Access
"Lessons for SEL" YouTube Channel	https://bit.ly/EASELlessons	

Explore the resources available on the Casel website at www.casel.org. First, digest the "Fundamentals of SEL" section to help you understand what SEL actually is and how it benefits adults and students of all ages. Pay particular attention to the framework, Casel's interactive wheel, and commit to memory the five core skills and competencies: self-awareness, self-management, social awareness, relationship skills, and responsible decision-making. Later in the book, I'll dive deeply into each competency and how to help it come alive in both your personal and professional life. Going through these valuable resources will help you to answer the questions in the "Curiosity Zone".

TABLE 1.9 Link and QR code for the Casel website

Resource	Bitly Link to Access	QR Code to Access
Casel website	https://bit.ly/EASELcasel	

Also, visit the Edutopia website at www.edutopia.org. This is a free website founded by the George Lucas Foundation in 1991. Edutopia conducts research and shines a spotlight on what is working in education. They are a trusted source. Go to the search box and just type in "social emotional learning". Find a few articles that sound interesting and check them out. Here, you will find actionable strategies you can adopt and use in your space to help SEL come alive for yourself and your students. You'll enjoy resources to support SEL for learners of all ages in various settings as well as Adult SEL.

TABLE 1.10 Link and QR code for the Edutopia website

Resource	Bitly Link to Access	QR Code to Access
Edutopia website	https://edut.to/3OslvcF	

I talked about this resource at length earlier in this chapter. You can really grow your knowledge and understanding by reading the LPI's Case Study "Preparing Teachers to Support Social and Emotional Learning" by Hannah Melnick and Lorea Martinez. I mentioned this resource above (in the "Supporting Social and Emotional Learning" section). It will provide you with a wealth of knowledge and understanding about how to bring SEL alive in your education space. It is so powerful!.

TABLE 1.11 Link and QR code for "Preparing Teachers to Support Social and Emotional Learning"

Resource	Bitly Link to Access	QR Code to Access
Learning Policy Institute: "*Preparing Teachers to Support Social and Emotional Learning*"	https://bit.ly/EASELlpi	

Explore Casel's "3 Signature Practices" on their website. This is an incredibly valuable tool that can help you plan and keep SEL at the forefront of your space. When you are here, you can plan, execute, and explain your SEL work to peers and friends and serve as a model to others. Here, you intentionally plan what SEL concepts you'll work on each day of the week and plan for integration of SEL into academics. You'll invite others into your classroom or learning community to share how you work in and with SEL. You'll also be aware of how you are nurturing, growing, and strengthening your own core SEL skills. You'll learn more strategies for SEL success to add to your own tool kit throughout this book even if you are in the Confidence Zone. I'll dive deeply into these practices in Chapter 8.

TABLE 1.12 Link and QR code for Casel's "3 Signature Practices"

Resource	Bitly Link to Access	QR Code to Access
Casel's *"3 Signature Practices Playbook"*	https://bit.ly/EASEL3signature	

 Reflection Questions

It's time to reflect on and process the information we are learning. Feel free to go back into the chapter to dig into some of these ideas. You can answer these questions by thinking about them, recording ideas in a journal, adding notes here, or creating audio or video notes.

TABLE 1.13 Link and QR code for the online reflection journal

\multicolumn{3}{l}{*I created an online tool with Google Jamboard that you can also access and use on your own if you'd like to. You can access it below. When you access the file, you'll be asked if you want to make a copy of the file. Say "yes" and this file will be in your Google Drive for you to use and refer back to throughout your reading of the text.*}
Resource	Bitly Link to Access	QR Code to Access
"Embracing Adult SEL" Google Jamboard Reflection Journal	https://bit.ly/EASELjournal1-4	

TABLE 1.14 Reflection question: Describe the fear, curiosity, confidence, and competence zones of SEL

Describe the fear, curiosity, confidence, and competence zones of SEL.			
Fear Zone	**Curiosity Zone**	**Confidence Zone**	**Competence Zone**

TABLE 1.15 Reflection question: What training and professional development in SEL have you had? This includes reading books and articles independently. What have you learned? Describe two ideas about SEL here

What training and professional development (PD) in SEL have you had? This includes reading books and articles independently. What have you learned? Describe two ideas about SEL here.	
SEL PD #1	**SEL PD #2**

TABLE 1.16 Reflection question: What zone are you in with respect to SEL? Explain how you know

What zone are you in with respect to SEL? Explain how you know.
Which zone are you in? Circle One.   Fear   Curiosity   Confidence   Competence
I know this because ....

TABLE 1.17 Reflection question: Is there someone on your team, at your school, or at your central office who serves as a local expert or facilitator or coach of SEL learning? If so, do you have a relationship with them? Do you feel comfortable approaching this person to engage in a conversation around SEL? Explain

Is there someone on your team, at your school, or at your central office who serves as a local expert or facilitator or coach of SEL learning? If so, do you have a relationship with him or her? Do you feel comfortable approaching this person to engage in a conversation around SEL? Explain.
Someone who could be helpful is ....

TABLE 1.18 Reflection question: What support do you need to foster SEL in your personal and professional life?

What support do you need to foster SEL in your personal and professional life?
I need ....

TABLE 1.19 Reflection question: What else are you thinking right now?

What else are you thinking right now about SEL?
I'm thinking ….

2

Establishing Your Adult SEL Practice
Embrace Proactive, Reactive, and Reflective Practices

A few years ago, I was asked to create a professional development module on Adult social emotional learning (SEL). In my training, I developed a three-part framework for identifying and practicing SEL skills on a personal level. The approach utilizes proactive, "in-the-moment", and reflective strategies for developing personal SEL skills or Adult SEL. I received feedback from participants who loved the approach. People shared that it was an organized and useful way to think about each area of SEL and that it helped them to feel empowered, not overwhelmed. One person connected their learning to having a "personal menu" for their SEL development. Let's dig into what that means on a deeper level.

By now, we know SEL is critically important to student success and improves academic outcomes; the research is clear on this. We also know that Adult SEL, or having the adults in education communities embrace, live, and model SEL skills, is a critical component of SEL implementation as well. When adults are skilled in SEL skills such as understanding their emotions, embracing their identities, and identifying their strengths and core values, it is much easier for them to support this same skill development in young people. Furthermore, when adults model these ideas, skills, and competencies in real time, students will have a much clearer idea of what SEL looks like and sounds like in the real world. SEL is the curriculum of life. Stand-alone lessons or online learning modules in SEL are helpful to explain concepts and grow knowledge, but we also need to show students how to do all of it authentically while they are living and learning. In order to do that, we have to embrace SEL ourselves.

Proactive Strategies

I love to analyze the meaning of words in my work. Proactive is defined here.

TABLE 2.1 Definition of proactive

Proactive	Acting in anticipation of **future problems**, needs, or changes

Being proactive helps us to be prepared for challenges that arise later. It's an investment. Muscle building. Synonyms of proactive include visionary and forward-looking. When we are proactive with any practice, we are building skills before they are needed, investing in the moment when we'll need to access them by creating skill muscles. This is a very manageable way to approach skill development. We can identify a habit or skill we know will help us be more prepared for a difficult moment, and we can practice it during a time of low stress. By doing this, we can be more prepared for a future problem or challenge. This has worked well for me in various situations, both personally and professionally.

An Everyday Challenge

One of my weaknesses is cooking. I am a terrible cook, and for some reason, I don't enjoy it at all. I have no idea why this is and have abandoned any vision of me enjoying cooking or being a skilled cook. My husband, on the other hand, actually unwinds when he gets home by cooking great meals! He relishes trying new and complex recipes, chopping lots of ingredients, and even creating a beautiful presentation of the food for us. I want no part of this! I am aware of what I enjoy around the house and how I relax. It might sound strange, but I enjoy tidying and organizing different areas of our home. I don't mind doing the laundry and smile with delight as a pile of dirty clothes in front of me shrinks in the process. Even weeding in the garden gives me a peaceful and fulfilled feeling. But cooking does not. I have a very high degree of self-awareness around this. I am also aware that my family of four needs to eat dinner every night, even when my husband is away, unavailable, or sick. So my proactive strategy for being able to function well in these moments is that I have two "go-to" recipes I can make for dinner. They are not complex and are certainly not the most sophisticated, but they work. I know how to execute them well, and at the end of the day, we will all be fed. One of them is breakfast for dinner. I can scramble and poach eggs, cook bacon, toast bread and bagels, and clean and assemble fruit. It's actually fun for all of us, and our two teenage children automatically say "Where's Dad?" when this option shows up. In a way, it's a special nod to my lack of skill, and I can embrace the moment and my weakness while I solve our problems. The other meal is grilled cheese. I harken back to my childhood when my mom made us grilled cheese for lunch, and I summon my meager skills to do the same. A grilled cheese sandwich at any time of day is always a hit! I can prepare a salad or a vegetable to go with it. I know we'll all be OK with this simple meal. Again, our kids smile when served another basic meal for dinner. I feel proud of myself when I successfully flip the sandwich in the pan, and we can all enjoy the moment when we bite into this classic.

My proactive approach is enormously helpful here! I can access my specific skills around making food without stress. I know how to do these two meals and do them well. I don't have to search for recipes or information online, in a cookbook or a cooking app, so I can stay positive, calm, and happy while I complete a task I don't usually do and I'm not very good at. If I were not prepared with my proactive approach and skills, these simple dinners might turn into a disaster.

We can proactively strengthen our SEL muscles by investing in practice that supports specific skill development. Habits are built with awareness and effort. By doing this, we can support a more calm and regulated state for ourselves which helps us to solve problems and support those around us whether it's our families, friends, and neighbors or our students or staff. Being proactive is a valuable skill that can also be taught to students and staff and modeled by example.

The *"Leader in Me"* program, based on the popular work of Steven Covey, the author of *The Seven Habits of Highly Effective People*, "is an evidence-based, comprehensive model that builds leadership and life skills in students, creates a high-trust school culture, and lays the foundation for sustained academic achievement." Their "mission is to unleash the greatness in students, educators, and school communities everywhere." It embraces habits as means of developing skills. Our school used these principles over the years; I recall Habit One in their curriculum as "Be Proactive". This is also the first concept I embrace in my quest to develop new competencies and skills, and it has been enormously helpful in my Adult SEL journey. This belief can also be applied to skills in one's professional and personal life. Once a practice takes hold authentically in one's toolbox, it's hard to separate when we will use it. In my practice, being proactive with skills is something I now do automatically without stopping to consider whether it's part of my personal or professional being. I work to do it in all aspects of my life. Embracing proactive practices is empowering in Adult SEL.

Proactive Strategies in the Classroom and the Schoolhouse

We use proactive strategies in the classroom all the time! It has long been written about and discussed that the moment a student enters a classroom is the most critical one of the class or the day. A proactive strategy for authentic connections with students and relationship building is our personal greeting. Educators are often asked or even required to be at the door to greet students. We've all seen incredible videos of educators who have individual greetings for students to meet their needs and see them on a personal level. They are so inspiring.

My greeting practice has evolved over the years. About five years ago, I changed where I was for my greeting. I noticed that when I was outside my door or in the hallway, I tended to focus on adults more by chatting with other teachers outside their doors instead of being authentically focused on the students entering my classroom. I also needed to be in my classroom to notice how each child was entering the room and starting their day. So I moved into my classroom, standing about 5 feet inside the doorway, next to our attendance chart. This way, I could greet each child personally in our classroom by name and then observe how they started their day. What was their demeanor like? Did they eat breakfast? Were they filled with energy or sluggish? Did they skip, stomp, or slink into the classroom? Were they being social with other students or quiet and shy? Did this change on a day-to-day basis? What kind of activities were they choosing to start their day? Was it something active like doing a puzzle, or were they quietly reading? Did they put their head down to rest or focus on their breakfast? All of this was non-verbal information, data really, for me about how my students were doing, and it helped me get ready to meet their needs. I could also be responsive to any problems or challenges that came up first thing in the morning. By thinking about my proactive practice and being open to changes with it, I was better able to meet my students' needs. Proactive practices can change, evolve, bloom, and grow. This is an important concept to hold onto with our SEL skill development.

How we welcome educators and staff into the schoolhouse matters too. A proactive practice of welcoming conditions can help foster connection, happiness, and positive emotions. This is a challenge as school leaders are often solving myriad problems just prior to welcoming students into the building when educators are arriving. So while it's not possible for school leaders to greet educators at the door personally every day, it's possible to create proactive welcoming rituals that foster connection and calm. This could include playing calm music over the loudspeaker for 30 minutes prior to student arrival. It could be a positive message of appreciation posted near a staff sign-in that is changed every day. Educators could have some system to anonymously or personally indicate their emotions that leaders can later consult to understand the pulse of the staff, so they can respond in a supportive way. Leaders can make a pre-student arrival announcement over the school intercom system to wish educators well for the day and show appreciation for their presence. Often overlooked, strategies that we use with our students can be some of the best supports and strategies for connecting with and validating our staff. A proactive approach works here too.

In-the-Moment Strategies

At times, our proactive practices can be inadequate to address situations as they arise throughout the day. In these times, we need to access "in-the-moment" strategies to help us get through the situation in a positive way.

The Merriam-Webster online dictionary definition of moment is here.

TABLE 2.2 Definition of moment

Moment	Present *time*

Being present is a necessity and a challenge in today's world. We are more distracted than ever by various forces, including the news, our phones, notifications, social media, email inboxes, deadlines, chores, as well as our worries and fears.

When problems arise in the moment, it's smart to slow down and access a strategy we have for handling a problem as it's occurring, in real time. As we work to be proactive with SEL skill development in our personal and professional lives, it's also wise to develop "in the moment" strategies. At the heart of these strategies is the need to slow down in the moment and really see and feel what is happening. We can think about this as being responsive vs. reactive. When we slow down and respond, the outcome will usually be more positive than when we react to the situation. For this to work well, we'll benefit from having tried-and-true "in-the-moment" strategies we can easily access when needed.

The Everyday Challenge

I'm going to revisit my lack of ability in cooking. This is something that can be a problem in my life. At times, as a woman, I almost feel as though it's my dirty little secret. To be a female and a mom and not like to cook or bake can induce shame. However, I'm committed to noticing this problem, not judging it, and finding a path forward when I am faced with this situation. As I explained earlier, my proactive approach to dealing with the fact that I may have to make dinner is to have two go-to meals at the ready when they are needed. As they are both alternatives to a more traditional dinner, they end up being fun for me to prepare and for my kids to eat. I can access my strategy when I have advance notice around my husband not being home or being able to prepare dinner, and it works out. But there are also scenarios to consider when this problem arrives unannounced. I may find out about this at the last minute, and we may be out of eggs and cheese, rendering my go-to recipes useless. If this happens on an evening when I am particularly spent from my day or facing a great deal of stress due to another problem, this could be a trigger moment. I could react with anger and frustration and unintentionally take that out on my kids. Confused, they may look at me like I'm crazy because I'm yelling at them even though they have absolutely nothing to do with the situation at hand! Enter my in-the-moment strategy. I simply order a pizza. I don't put pressure on myself to cook something just for the sake of cooking. I don't try to make something I have no confidence with to prove a point. This may actually backfire, as I burn or over- or under-cook the food and it ends up getting wasted. I just say "I'm going to order a pizza". It's easy and simple and will harm no one. That's my simple in-the-moment strategy for when I need to cook and my proactive strategy won't work. I forgive myself for being a bad cook, secure food for myself and my children, and we move on. If we have pizza two nights in a row, that's OK too. It's a great decision to use this strategy instead of allowing negative emotions to take over the scenario or to make too much of it. With this strategy, I've effectively reframed this moment into an opportunity to have a pizza night. I've changed the way I look at the facts and circumstances of the moment and quickly made a decision that made sense and doesn't contribute to a negative outcome.

In-the-Moment Strategies in Action

Some days after my welcoming ritual, I notice I need to make adjustments to create the best learning conditions for me and my students for the day. For example, I have noticed that student energy just seems to lag on some days. Students are just more sluggish on some days than others. The down energy vibe seems to be magnified when the weather is cloudy or rainy and after days off and particularly on Mondays. This can make engaging students in learning a challenge. It could be for any number of reasons. Students most likely stay up late on the weekends. They could spend lots of time on screens and playing video games. Maybe their meal schedule has been out of whack after the predictability of breakfast and lunch in school all week, which makes coming in with energy on a Monday morning difficult. Rain may bring on emotions that are downbeat or difficult. There are infinite possibilities. When I see this happening, I can notice it without judgment and I can make decisions in the moment to create a joyful and energetic vibe when I feel that we need it after our regular community-building routines. I may decide to start the class or the day with a fun game such as "Don't Say 12" or a "Rock, Paper, Scissors" Tournament. I can also have a check-in that asks "What's on your mind?" or "How are you feeling today?" for our connection activity. Brain breaks can be energy up vs. energy down for the class or day. I can also modify academic activities to promote connection by offering choices to work together vs. quiet, individual activities. On Tuesdays, when my students seem to erupt with energy, I do the same thing except maybe I am incorporating activities into our learning that work to channel that energy in a positive way and bring it down. It's important to really notice moments and lean into change when needed. Having a toolkit of "in-the-moment" strategies is enormously helpful.

Reflective Strategies

One of the most powerful tools we can access is our metaphorical rearview mirror and the images we see as we engage in the act of reflection after the fact. We can learn so much about ourselves and everyday situations when we embrace reflective strategies.

TABLE 2.3 Definition of reflection

Reflection	The production of an image by or as if by a **mirror**

After things play out in our personal and professional lives, it's a powerful practice to reflect on them both when things went poorly as well as when they turned out well. The key to this strategy is making the time and space for the reflection and committing to doing it. This can be a challenge. Great times to do this are the beginning and the end of the day as most of our days are packed with constant activity and decision-making, especially as educators and school leaders. I long ago concluded that I most likely won't give time and space to reflection during the school day since being present as an educator and executing my job as a teacher take every fiber of my being. My mind is filled with plans, information I am processing in real time about my students, micro-decisions that result in changes to plans, the emotions of the young people and adults around me as well as the steady stream of requests via email, Class Dojo, text message, and more. If I do have time to reflect during the day, it may not be thorough or even accurate if it's still swathed in emotion around what happened or if my mind is very full. The end of the day is also a challenge for me as I am much more of a morning person. At the end of the school day, I am usually spent. So I notice that without judgment and intentionally schedule my reflection time in light of this fact. On my way home, I often open the windows and just breathe vs. listening to music or a podcast. I need that quiet time to regroup for the rest of my day. I want to rejuvenate when I get home so I can be present for evening activities with my family, so that becomes a priority over deep reflection. Because of this, a lot of my reflection happens the next day and I am OK with that. Reflecting is part of my mindful morning practice. I have great flow in the morning and much more energy, so that is where I create space for reflection, particularly when I have struggled with a situation and know I could have done better. My reflective strategy is to determine the root cause of my failure or success and then see if I can change or replicate the conditions around the event. Finding the time that works for you to embrace this practice will allow you the opportunity to deeply reflect and move forward armed with the benefit of that process.

Everyday Examples

Here are some personal and professional everyday examples of reflection I have engaged in that have revealed quite a bit to me.

Scenario 1: I caused my teenage daughter stress. When my daughter was having trouble with friends, I caused her additional stress. She eventually told me to leave her alone when I was trying to help her out. This broke my heart. After reflecting on what happened, I realized I expressed my concern for her in an unhelpful way. I was focused on my emotions instead of hers. I asked questions that did not help, and I gave her unsolicited advice. I failed to listen or use empathy and never considered her perspective, causing her to shut down. Once I realized this, I read a few articles and watched some videos about providing empathetic support and developed a list of questions I could ask her in the future that would be more helpful to her. I'll go into this in detail in Chapter 5. My ability to be authentically supportive increased dramatically. After failing, I reflected and grew and got better at providing her with support.

Scenario 2: I didn't help out at school when I was asked. After being asked to cover someone's class one morning, I said no in an extremely unhelpful way. I was so upset about my behavior and reaction that I deeply reflected later that day to really think about what happened. I realized that I had been told I would have to do this first thing in the morning by someone I didn't have a strong relationship with. I first thought of myself instead of the other person. I did not empathize with them or their situation and furthermore was exhausted as this happened on a Friday morning at the end of the week when I was tired. I didn't reframe the situation, and I abandoned my core values. As a result, I was less than helpful or kind. By identifying the root causes of this situation, I was able to avoid another one like it in the future.

Scenario 3: I didn't make the time I wanted to achieve in a running race. I did not train properly. I abandoned my training plan halfway through it and ran only twice a week instead of four times per week. The day before the race, I worked at a volunteer event all day and was on my feet for six hours. I wasn't properly hydrated. I realized some of the root causes were in my control and some were out of my control. Armed with this knowledge, I understood the path to greater success next time and was eventually able to achieve my running goal!

Scenario 4: I cooked a terrible meal. Back to this problem. When I had to cook dinner on my own, instead of relying on my in-the-moment strategy, I forged ahead on my own and tried a new recipe. I tried to be fancy. I burned food that resulted in waste and left all of us hungry, so we eventually had to order out. I reflected and realized that I was so wrapped up in my insecurity about cooking that I wasn't present or focused when I was trying to follow the directions for the meal. I employed a fixed mindset and was negative about the situation from the moment I started. I also didn't plan out the meal at all. All of this negativity and stress resulted in me not being able to perform. Upon reflection, I realized that if I am going to cook, an activity that I am deeply insecure about, I need to plan well and be prepared; otherwise, it will likely not go very well. Now this is what I think about before I cook a meal, and it helps me avoid failure.

Reflective Strategies in Action

Although it can be hard to find the time to reflect after spending a day teaching in a classroom or running a school, it's vital for us to engage our rearview mirror mentality and analyze why we were successful and why we failed. This process provides us with valuable data and information that can help us be more successful in the future. With practice, this will become automatic as our muscles grow. In the schoolhouse, many everyday scenarios provide opportunities to practice this thinking and build up our reflection skills. Here are some great situations for educators and leaders to think about:

> ★ A conversation or interaction that left everyone smiling
> ★ A lesson that went extremely well or extremely poorly
> ★ A routine that helped you feel good and up to a challenge
> ★ Positive or negative interactions with co-workers or families
> ★ Particularly invigorating or exhausting days
> ★ Successful or unsuccessful staff meetings
> ★ Effective or ineffective meetings of professional learning communities
> ★ Schoolwide initiatives that were a hit or failed to make the mark
> ★ Community engagement efforts that engaged or empowered families vs. those with little participation or drastically varying participation by different subgroups
> ★ An awful or really enjoyable family meal or activity
> ★ Professional Development that everyone raves about

When we internalize and commit to the proactive, in-the-moment, and reflective strategy model, we are investing in our ability to work successfully through challenges with skill, not just emotion. Difficult situations can trigger intense emotions which can be hard to work through and deter us from doing our job in meeting the needs of our students and staff. Armed with skills, we'll see different outcomes that are better and more positive so we can celebrate, savor, and replicate them. We'll use this model for SEL skill development throughout our learning journey together.

What's Next?

In my work with adult learners around SEL, I have found that many people need a path to follow, a roadmap to success. This can be hard to articulate clearly as the idea of SEL is massive, all-encompassing, and so important that it's easy to get overwhelmed. Curriculum for students helps us teach kids about SEL, but it doesn't meet the need to develop Adult SEL at the same time. Embracing the Casel model of five core skills is a great way to approach one's learning. It's critical to remember that these five core skills apply to both students and adults; they are not just for kids. They are for us too. When we lean into our own skill development and commit to embracing the skills, growing our competency in them through practice and vulnerability, and modeling them in real time, magical things happen. Students will understand SEL in an incredibly powerful way, and we'll enjoy their learning and growth right before our very own eyes as we grow in SEL. But remember, the journey starts with us.

Now that we understand the proactive, in-the-moment, and reflective strategy model, we can apply this to SEL skill development in an organized fashion. We can do this in an intentional way to build up our SEL skills. People need an understandable approach, and some will benefit by looking at the skills individually as well as collectively. The five core skills of self-awareness, self-management, social awareness, relationship skills, and responsible decision-making have overlapping and complementary elements. Our skills in some areas affect our skills in others. It's critical for us to find an entry point, a starting place in our SEL learning.

If we want to be successful human beings, we have to be able to function well in all different types of settings, conditions, and situations. This means we have to make good decisions in the various parts of our life. By building up our SEL skills, we can arrive at that point of synthesis, of responsible decision-making when we put together all of the work in the rest of the skill areas. The base layer of all of these skills is self-awareness. Think of self-awareness as the foundation of ourselves. When it's strong, secure, and deeply understood, we can work on additional skills that will benefit us in our personal and professional lives. Once we have self-awareness, we can develop the ability to manage ourselves. This is so critical for success!

Self-management skills help us move through the various situations we encounter on any given day at home, in the world, and in our places of work: schools and classrooms. Once we build our base with strong skills around self, we move outward to others. This is where social awareness comes in. It can be difficult to achieve great social awareness without this base and foundational knowledge and understanding of ourselves created with intentional work around self-awareness. With greater understanding of ourselves, our blind spots become visible and we can address them. With our eyes wide open, we can appreciate others' experiences, cultures, backgrounds, and perspectives as our social awareness grows. Then, when we activate and embrace a broader perspective, we can understand and appreciate complex issues and challenges in society and arrive at a place of action in empathy.

Relationships appear and grow in this space. As we understand ourselves more authentically and completely and work to manage ourselves in a variety of situations and employ social awareness, people are drawn to us. We can create and nurture positive relationships with a variety of people. In schools and classrooms, this means we can connect successfully with students, families, co-workers, and peers as well as the broader community. We can also recognize negative relationships that are no longer working for us and be brave enough to trim them from our lives. When we do this, we'll enjoy the ability to make better decisions in all types of situations. In Figure 2.1, you can see what this approach looks like, starting with self-awareness and working our way up with our skills.

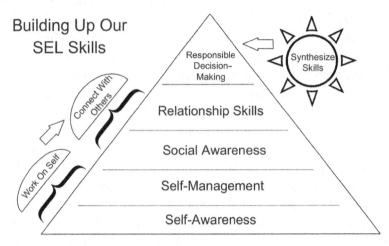

Figure 2.1 Building up our SEL skills.

With greater skills, we can enjoy more success. An organized approach can foster skill development and eventually SEL competence in a way that is accessible and makes sense. If we are not self-aware, it will be difficult to manage ourselves or use social awareness. It may also be very difficult to build and sustain positive relationships or make good decisions. Conversely, when we invest in understanding and embracing our true and authentic selves, use self-management strategies, and commit to being socially aware, we'll enjoy a variety of positive relationships. At this point, we can use all of our skills to make great decisions and be more successful human beings. When we build up our SEL skills, we are on the road to success.

 Reflection Questions

It's time to reflect on and process the information we are learning. Feel free to go back into the chapter to dig into some of these ideas. You can answer these questions by thinking about them, recording ideas in a journal, adding notes here, or creating audio or video notes.

TABLE 2.4 Link and QR Code for the online reflection journal

I created an online tool with Google Jamboard that you can also access and use on your own if you'd like to. You can access it below. When you access the file, you'll be asked if you want to make a copy of the file. Say "yes" and this file will be in your Google Drive for you to use and refer back to throughout your reading of the text.		
Resource	**Bitly Link to Access**	**QR Code to Access**
"Embracing Adult SEL" Google Jamboard Reflection Journal	*https://bit.ly/EASEL journal1-4*	

TABLE 2.5 Reflection Question: Explain the difference between proactive, in-the-moment, and reflective strategies

Explain proactive, in-the-moment, and reflective strategies.		
Proactive Strategies	**In-the-Moment Strategies**	**Reflective Strategies**

TABLE 2.6 Reflection Question: identify an everyday challenge in your life and specific strategies you can use to address it that are proactive, in-the-moment, and reflective, as in my example of cooking

Identify an everyday challenge in your life and specific strategies you can use to address it that are proactive, in-the-moment, and reflective, as in my example of cooking. *The challenge is _____.*		
Proactive Strategies	**In-the-Moment Strategies**	**Reflective Strategies**

TABLE 2.7 Reflection Question: How would you like to approach building your five core SEL skills?

How would you like to approach building your five core SEL competencies?
I'd like to ….

TABLE 2.8 Reflection question: Does this organized approach seem like one that could work for you? Why or why not?

Does this organized approach seem like one that could work for you? Why or why not?
This seems like …

TABLE 2.9 Reflection Question: What else are you thinking right now?

What else are you thinking right now about the idea of proactive, in-the-moment, and reflective strategies?
I'm thinking ...

3

Leaning Into Ourselves

Start Your SEL Journey with Self-Awareness

I have been happily married for almost 20 years. I can't believe I can actually say that. I am a child of divorce. I didn't have a strong model of what a successful relationship looked like growing up, and I knew it. My parents' divorce was final when I was 16 years old, but as a younger child, I had a Spidey sense, a feeling that something was off long before my parents split up. I was aware. That awareness helped me to deal with the split when it occurred since it wasn't a surprise for me. I think I always had hoped it would work, but I knew it wouldn't. My understanding of this was strong. As an adult, I had trouble developing trusting relationships in the dating world in my 20s. I knew the reason why, but for years I wouldn't face it. Finally, in my early 30s, I worked with a therapist and figured all of this out. I knew I had to change if I was going to make a relationship work. More than anything, I wanted to have a family, a happy life with a partner and children. I met my eventual husband on my 32nd birthday, and we are blessed and fortunate to have two healthy kids and a great life together.

We are one of those couples whose personalities complement each other. We have similar values, goals, and some interests but differ in how we are in some big ways. I am more social, an energetic morning person, and I enjoy energy and activity more than not. This can be music, laughter, conversation, and even the great outdoors. But I struggle with quiet at times. Upon examination, I realize that quiet, growing up, could mean something negative. It might mean someone was in a bad mood and it could be taken out on you in a flash, or it might mean no one was around to hang out with or help you.

My family growing up was decidedly not quiet for the most part, and what has stayed with me is that when it was quiet, it was more likely that things were more bad than good. That understanding of quiet has stayed with me and impacts me today. I have very strong self-awareness around this.

My husband Dan is an amazing person. He is calm, consistent, and dependable. Unflappable you might say. He is a "steady Eddie". This nicely balances my energy and myriad emotions. He grew up in a family that was, quite simply, quiet. So, he is, at times, very quiet. He loves to read and cook and will do so in silence. If I attempt to cook, I prefer noise in the background or people with me. Embracing teaching as a career has kept me surrounded by people constantly, and I have really enjoyed that social aspect of my job. So I've had to learn over the years that when my husband is quiet, that does not mean trouble. I understand this completely now, but it was a journey to get here.

Through deep self-awareness and understanding of myself, I have come to understand that quiet can be a trigger for me, something that can initiate an uncomfortable emotional state that may include annoyance, fear, or discomfort. I struggled with that in the early days of our marriage. I would repeatedly ask my husband if something was wrong. Almost all of the time, his answer was a simple no. I annoyed him with all of the asking. His reassurances helped, but an uncomfortable feeling gnaws at me still some days. The difference now is that I know what to do about it. When things feel too quiet, I get up and move. I text a friend or call my sister. I work on a puzzle or wipe down the kitchen counters. I walk the dog or fold laundry. I address my feelings calmly and in a way that makes sense. My self-awareness led me to this place of acceptance and action.

Having self-awareness around this trigger and the related feelings has given me the power to engage in strategies to manage it without damaging our relationship or spiraling into something worse. Without this deep analysis of myself, I would not be able to handle these moments well, and it could have a negative impact on our relationship. This is an important example of adult social emotional learning (SEL) in my personal life around the skill of self-awareness.

What Is Self-Awareness?

Let's head back to the dictionary to construct some meaning out of this phrase.

TABLE 3.1 Definitions of self and awareness

Self	An **individual's** *typical* **character** *or* **behavior**
Awareness	**Knowledge and understanding** *that something is happening or exists*

From these meanings, we can put together a definition that might sound like "an individual's knowledge and understanding of their own character and behavior".

Self-awareness is all about deeply examining and understanding ourselves. When we better understand ourselves, we can harness the power we have to make change, achieve goals, impact situations around us, and learn and grow. At times, it means interrogating ourselves and our beliefs, challenging them when needed. It's introspection, reflection, and understanding. And it's necessary for us to engage in if we are to grow our SEL skills and model them for others. Our Adult SEL journey starts with self-awareness.

Casel defines self-awareness as "the abilities to understand one's own emotions, thoughts, and values and how they influence behavior across contexts. This includes capacities to recognize one's strengths and limitations with a well-grounded sense of confidence and purpose." Self-awareness helps us identify and think deeply about our values, strengths and weaknesses, emotions, thoughts and feelings, identities in various settings, our mindset, and interests as well as prejudices and biases. This helps us develop a sense of purpose and map out priorities in our personal and professional lives as well as supports our development as a whole person so we can connect with others. Let's explore strategies to support our self- awareness. With this work, we are in the Confidence Zone of SEL, understanding how to engage in strategies that support our skill development and help us live in SEL.

Proactive Strategies for Self-Awareness

Identify your strengths. We all possess various qualities that make us who we are, and some of them are more developed than others, meaning we are stronger in them. When we adopt a strength-based mindset about ourselves, we focus on what we can do well and then connect that to our dreams and goals so we are successful. If we focus on our weaknesses and what we are not skilled in, we can get mired in negative thinking and even spend too much time worrying about or focus on skills that don't support our goals and dreams. So how do we focus on identifying our strengths? We can brainstorm a list of ideas, but more powerful insights can be found by using tools developed specifically for this purpose.

One reliable and easy-to-use tool I love is the VIA Character Survey. This free online survey asks a series of questions to identify your top strengths from a list of 24 character traits.

TABLE 3.2 Link and QR code for the VIA character survey

Resource	Link to Access	QR Code to Access
VIA Character Survey	https://bit.ly/EASELvia	

Developed by psychologists, the survey takes about five minutes to complete, and you can view a report of your strengths for free. VIA organizes the character traits they focus on into six big ideas.

TABLE 3.3 VIA character strengths

Wisdom	Courage	Humanity	Justice	Temperance	Transcendence
Creativity	Bravery	Kindness	Fairness	Forgiveness	Appreciation of beauty and excellence
Curiosity	Honesty	Love	Leadership	Humility	Gratitude
Judgment	Perseverance	Social intelligence	Teamwork	Prudence	Hope
Love of learning	Zest			Self-regulation	Humor
Perspective					Spirituality

I have actually taken this assessment twice, both in 2020 near the beginning of the pandemic and again in 2023. It's interesting to see how my list has both evolved and showed consistency over time.

TABLE 3.4 Results of author's character strengths surveys

My Top Character Traits in 2020	My Top Character Traits in 2023
Love of learning	Gratitude
Curiosity	Hope
Gratitude	Appreciation of beauty and excellence
Creativity	Zest
Appreciation of beauty and excellence	Honesty

This list makes sense to me. I have grown my gratitude practice intentionally since the pandemic entered our lives. I've also had to embrace hope in a big way in light of challenges that we have faced as a family and that the world has faced and continues to face as I write this. Seeing many injustices play out in front of our eyes since 2020 has motivated me to be more honest about what I believe and what is right. Teaching through the pandemic has challenged me to solve problems through innovation in a way I didn't know was possible. This challenge and the growth I have experienced in using technology, fostering relationships, and meeting students' needs have been incredibly powerful and rewarding. I have always been aware of the power of physical beauty and its ability to calm and motivate us in both big and small ways. I regularly stop to see natural beauty whenever and however I can, and I work to share it with others. The appearance of zest on my list is validation of my approach to life. I get to live life and experience adventures on a daily basis. With energy, I approach opportunities and challenges in ways that help me to navigate them. At the same time, there are traits I'd like to see higher up on my list of top traits. I can use this data to help me hone skills in other areas as well. Personally, I want to grow my strength in the Humanity and Temperance traits. I plan to do the survey again to see my progress.

Embracing a strength-based approach in ourselves makes sense. In the fantastic book *Hacking Deficit Thinking*, authors Dr. Byron McClure and Dr. Kelsie Reed share "A strength based approach helps people learn to use their strong points, skills, talents, and abilities to face challenges, resolve conflicts, design innovative solutions and change the world. It focuses on developing a person's unique strengths" (McClure and Reed, 2022, p. 27). The very first step in this process for ourselves is to investigate and reflect on our strengths. You can access outstanding resources for getting started with a strength-based approach at the website supporting the book, https://www.strengthbasedcollective.com/. I also highly recommend reading *Hacking Deficit Thinking* by Dr. McClure and Dr. Reed to learn more about strength-based approaches.

TABLE 3.5 Link and QR code for strength-based collective

Resource	Link to Access	QR Code to Access
Strength-Based Collective	https://bit.ly/EASELstrength	

Embrace your identity and culture. Merriam-Webster's definition of **identity** is here.

TABLE 3.6 Definition of identity

| *Identity* | The **distinguishing** *character or personality of an individual* |

It's critical that we, as human beings who navigate various roles and responsibilities in different settings on a daily basis, understand our distinguishing characteristics and personality to better understand ourselves. Part of the ability to do so is to understand and identify the various elements of our identity. A useful tool for doing this is an identity wheel. Creating an identity wheel for yourself is a valuable exercise in self-awareness. Going through this process can help you paint a clearer picture of your whole self, necessary for developing this SEL skill.

When teams create and share identity wheels, they create connection points among people and the process normalizes vulnerability. When we share our authentic selves, we give a little piece of us to others and to our community. That act alone can go a long way in building connection, appreciation, and trust and works well in any community, including schools and classrooms.

There are many versions of identity wheels. The main idea to understand is that they are flexible and fluid. They can hold any number of traits, including pieces of our identity that are fixed and others that may be in flux or are evolving. The visual can help you think about and create your own identity wheel to help you understand and reflect on exactly who you are.

Figure 3.1 Elements of identity and identity wheel template.

Identity and culture are deeply related. Let's define **culture**.

TABLE 3.7 Definition of identity

Culture	The customary **beliefs**, *social forms, and material* **traits** *of a* **racial, religious, or social group**

In a diverse world, we know that in any space we share with others, there could be vastly different customs, social rituals, and ideas around many aspects of our lives. A critical resource for helping me understand culture in a powerful way is the work of Zaretta Hammond in *Culturally Responsive Teaching & The Brain*. Her definition of culture identifies three distinct levels of culture.

Surface level culture – Observable and concrete elements, including food, dress, music, and holidays. This level of culture has a low emotional charge.

(Hammond, 2015, p. 22)

Shallow culture – The unspoken rules around everyday social interactions and norms. This includes ideas around being late, eye contact, positioning of family members in roles of importance or reverence, attitudes toward elder family members, personal space, and touching as well as body language and non-verbal communication. This level of culture has a strong emotional charge. Practices that differ from our own can be interpreted as hostile, threatening, or disrespectful.

(Hammond, 2015, p. 22)

Deep culture – These are the deep beliefs we hold. It is made up of both pieces of knowledge and unconscious assumptions we have about important ideas such as our ethics and morals, spirituality, child-rearing practices, and group harmony. These elements of culture have an intense emotional charge as opposition to them can create a sense of threat and result in a fight, flight, or freeze response.

(Hammond, 2015, p. 23)

Because of the complexity of culture and the fact that different elements of culture can create strong responses that may impact relationships, it's a smart move to understand our own culture on these three levels. Once we do this, we can identify blind spots and work to understand practices that differ from our own, so we can develop the skills to connect with, work with, and relate to others who have different cultural practices. This is particularly critical in education as we work with students and staff from a wide variety of backgrounds and experiences. This exercise in self-awareness is an investment in our ability to understand ourselves deeply. In her text, Ms. Hammond says: "people often represent the three levels of culture as an iceberg, with surface culture as the tip of the iceberg, shallow culture located just below the water line, and deep culture the largest part hidden deep in the water" (Hammond, 2015, pp. 23–24). This could look something like this.

Figure 3.2 Levels of culture iceberg model.

The shallow level of culture is particularly thought-provoking as some behaviors and actions may be observable but the beliefs around them are not, which can result in misunderstandings and even judgment. In the text, there is a beautiful and powerful illustration comparing culture to a tree. I highly recommend reading *"Culturally Responsive Teaching & The Brain"* by Zaretta Hammond to learn more.

Identify your blind spots. All human beings have implicit bias whether we realize it or not. What does it mean exactly?

TABLE 3.8 Definition of implicit bias

Implicit bias	A **prejudice** *that is* **present** *but* **not consciously held or recognized**

Implicit bias and these prejudices are deeply seated in our brains and live below the conscious level, so we may not be aware of them. They can govern how we think and act with respect to groups of people on the basis of race, class, gender, and abilities as well as other identity markers and more often against marginalized groups. Our own experiences and identities can make it hard for us to spot when we are biased because we are grounded in our own thinking and experiences, not the experiences of others. Additionally, implicit bias can run counter to our expressed beliefs. An example of this is someone who maintains that they accept all humans as equals but look down on someone in a certain job or who is from a lower socioeconomic background. Where we come from, our backgrounds, and beliefs all shape and contribute to our implicit biases. While we can't eliminate the biases we have, we can work to be self-aware about them and that helps us to identify our blind spots so we can work against them.

A free and useful tool is the Project Implicit website from Harvard University.

TABLE 3.9 Link and QR code for Harvard University Project Implicit website

Resource	Link to Access	QR Code to Access
Harvard University Project Implicit	https://bit.ly/EASELimplicit	

The website has many different Implicit Association Tests, or IATs. This online resource allows you to answer questions that will help you understand if you have implicit biases with regard to race, gender, sexual orientation, ability, and more. It is useful, insightful, and incredibly easy to use. It may help you uncover your implicit biases so you can identify blind spots and work specifically against them. Here are some examples:

- A person who works in the retail industry identifies they have a bias against elderly people.
- A fit person comes to understand they are biased against overweight people.
- A person of Christian faith has implicit bias around those who celebrate religious holidays and culture in communities that are Jewish, Muslim, Hindu, and Indigenous.
- A teacher comes to understand they believe male students are more suited for science and math projects.
- An educator realizes they have bias against certain races, believing some are not geared for honors courses and accelerated learning opportunities and are more prone to behavior challenges.

Taking at least three of these tests and revisiting the process over time (for example, yearly) will help you create self-awareness that can be addressed in both your personal and professional life.

Identify your core values. After spending 12 years in the classroom, I entered a period of transition in my professional life. I started to write this book and was building an education consulting business. My emotions were up and down on a daily basis, so I sought support in many different ways. One of them was to read *Always Strive to Be a Better You* by Pete Hall. I met Pete and Kristin Souers, the authors of *Fostering Resilient Learners*, at a professional development session they led in Delaware in 2018 on childhood trauma. I eventually joined their team as a professional development facilitator and continue to value their perspective, support, and wisdom. Pete's book came out in late 2022 at the perfect time for me when I needed to stay strong and stay the course with my newest professional goals.

Around the same time, I attended a webinar on "Transformational Professional Development" given by Bright Morning Consulting, founded by Elena Aguilar. Ms. Aguilar is an expert in coaching and emotional intelligence. I love her work and its strong, clear ties to SEL. As the facilitator started the webinar, she shared about herself as well as three of her core values to start the session. I was struck by this moment! It was deeply personal and vulnerable yet powerful and strong and so simple. It immediately provided an opportunity for connection and respect. I made a note to incorporate this practice into my own professional development sessions going forward.

Later that day, I was at home reading Pete's book. Chapter 2 is called "Strengthen Your Core". One of the exercises in the chapter is to identify your core values by using a rating scale on 100 different values. This was a second sign to think about core values. Part of our self-awareness is to identify and lean into our core values. I completed the activity in the book and identified five core values. It was incredibly hard to narrow down the list to just five, but I came up with joy, creativity, impact, growth, and kindness. You can use a simple process to identify your core values with Pete's book or with the article "6 Ways to Discover and Choose Your Core Values" from *Psychology Today*.

TABLE 3.10 Link and code for "6 Ways to Discover and Choose Your Core Values"

Resource	Link to Access	QR Code to Access
Article: *"6 Ways to Discover and Choose Your Core Values"*	https://bit.ly/EASELcore	

It is great to know and articulate our core values. However, we can take it a step further and activate our core values by living them. Doing this exercise in Pete's book helped me focus on the idea that if a project or activity I am working on or being asked to do does not support my core values, I should reevaluate whether or not I should do it, especially during a time of transition. I can say no and that's OK.

Last year, I was asked to lead a Tree Preservation Committee in my neighborhood. I was immediately thinking that this would be a bad idea despite its being a topic of interest and passion for me. I was still a full-time teacher, the challenges in the classroom were significant, and I was facing burnout. How could I possibly add another thing to my plate? However, upon further consideration, I realized that this was the perfect activity for me. Spending time in the natural world brings me joy. Holding an education event around the benefit of trees and organizing a tree planting event in my community created a positive impact on my community. Donating my time to a cause and the not-for-profit partner we collaborated with, the Delaware Center for Horticulture, was an act of kindness. I used creativity to build learning materials and schedule our in-person event and experienced growth when I connected with new members of our community and learned exactly how to plant a tree! It was all in direct alignment with my core values, so it was a win to say yes to the opportunity when my first instinct was to say no. By saying yes to this opportunity despite a busy schedule, I was actually living my core values. Activating our core values can help us find clarity in what we do personally and professionally.

Write a "Where I'm From" poem. A simple yet powerful tool to help us express our complex identity is a "Where I'm From" poem. A well-known version of this type of poem is by Kentucky poet laureate George Ella Lyon. In her "Where I'm From" poem, she speaks of her family, her surroundings, childhood memories, and hobbies as well as family mantras. It is a beautiful and authentic way to begin to share oneself with others as well as work creatively with language to express personal thoughts and feelings by creating vivid imagery. I just love it.

TABLE 3.11 Link and QR code for "Where I'm From" poem

Resource	Link to Access	QR Code to Access
Poem: *"Where I'm From"* by George Ella Lyon	https://bit.ly/EASELwhere	

I learned about this type of poetry after it was mentioned in two different professional learning sessions I attended in 2021, both about building culturally aware and responsive learning spaces. Again it was a sign! It can be adapted for any age and is a powerful tool in self-awareness and expression. I did this exercise in one of the sessions and as a model for my students. Here is my poem.

Where I'm From
By Mrs. Turner

I am from orange shag carpet in the TV room and records playing in the house
A round kitchen table set for six and Toasty the cat
I am from ice cream cones, frozen pizza, grapefruit with sugar, and goulash
And the slate floor in the hallway with stairs all the way up to floor three

I am from azalea bushes, a porch with screen, and wiffle ball games
A tire swing out front and bikes with banana seats
Japanese beetle traps in the yard, washing cars in the driveway, shoveling snow
And lightning bugs at dusk, dirty feet after warm summer days.

I am from the woodsy path behind the lake house going down to Elm Beach
And swimming pools and BBQs and baseball games in the city
I'm from travel near and far, young and old
I'm from shuttling between two homes and forgetting things. Heartbreak.

Figure 3.3 Author's "Where I'm From" poem, part 1.

I am from Sandy and Richie, two sisters and a bro
With Grandmas, Grandpas, Aunt Bobbi, Uncle Tom, Aunt Mary, cousins near & far
I am from "You can always count on your family", New Jersey, Upstate New York
Being called the wrong name by mom. And more heartbreak.

I am from holiday dinners and frozen yogurt pie
Popcorn on the stove with melted butter and home movies
I am from big boxes of summer and winter clothes drug from the attic
Keds, Guess jeans, Firenza sweaters and Kenya bags
Record players, radio stations, aimless car rides around town

I am from sticker albums, jewelry boxes, Cat's Cradle, Yahtzee, and card games.
And sisters. Sharing. Fighting. Curling irons and Sun-in
Learning how "not to throw like a girl".
I am from memories. Love and traditions all around me.

Figure 3.4 Author's "Where I'm From" poem, part 2.

Although the end result will look different for people of all ages, the intent and the power in the result are the same. It's an authentic expression of self that, when shared, will create community by revealing connections, vulnerability, and personal experiences. It helps us focus on the various elements of culture so individuals can feel seen, heard, and validated. It can help us reflect on our experiences and why we are how we are. Anyone can grow through this process of identifying and sharing their diverse backgrounds, cultures, and contexts by articulating the individual pieces of their culture and themselves. Sharing your culture and experiences with your community is powerful! Modeling vulnerable sharing is an authentic act that will help you build strong connections with others. When we identify and clearly see our differences as well as our commonalities, we can come together as human beings.

You can use this simple, online template to create your own "Where I'm From" poem. I did this recently with a group of educators at a professional development session on SEL while we were focusing on social awareness. When we gathered for our closing circle at the end of our time together, more than half of the participants shared that writing the poem was their favorite part of the day. Some even emailed it to their parents right away, bringing tears and lots of emotions. I was blown away by the power of this simple activity that celebrates identity and culture. Imagine the power of this in a classroom!

TABLE 3.12 Link and QR code to "Where I'm From" Writing Activity

Resource	Link to Access	QR Code to Access
Template: *"Where I'm From" Writing Activity*	https://bit.ly/EASELtemplate	

You can also read a blog I wrote for Savvas Learning on the power of using this poem to support student learning around identity in SEL. Please note, however, that this activity may be a difficult one for someone to complete if they come from challenging circumstances. It could trigger feelings that are unwelcome and uncomfortable. A way to support all participants in this activity is to offer a modification. One way this poem can be adapted is to offer the idea to create a "Where I Am" poem that takes the core ideas and articulates how they are visible in one's life today. Adults and students can also create a "Where I Am Going" poem to articulate a vision of where they would like to be and what that would look and sound like.

TABLE 3.13 Link and QR code to "Where I'm From" Writing Activity

Resource	Link to Access	QR Code to Access
Blog: *"Where I'm From" Writing Activity*	https://bit.ly/EASELwriting	

Learn how the brain works. I don't ever recall learning how our brain works or what was happening when I experienced big emotions as a child. I wish I had known what was going on. This is a critical part of our lives as human beings. Since I have worked for Kristin Souers and Pete Hall, the authors of *Fostering Resilient Learners*, I have become so much more knowledgeable about how the brain works. A big part of their work on mitigating the impacts of childhood trauma is to understand the impact of trauma on the brain and the science behind our emotions so we can empower kids and teachers with that knowledge and learn to work through and support our emotions, not avoid them or get stuck on them. I highly recommend reading their book *Fostering Resilient Learners*.

Our brain is a complex part of our nervous system and is responsible for so much. We need to understand how it works so we can work with it. Then we can pass this knowledge and information to others around us. Here is a basic description of the parts of the brain, how they work together, and what they are responsible for.

The **cerebrum** is the largest part of our brain and helps us think and speak. The **cerebellum** is a small part in the back of the brain and helps our muscles to coordinate movements and balance. Our **prefrontal cortex** is behind our foreheads and it helps us make plans and decisions. The **hippocampus** is at the center of the brain and works like a file cabinet to help us store and find memories. Finally, the **amygdala** is deep in the center of our brain and it controls our emotions. **Neurons** are tiny brain cells that make and send signals to other cells in the body, telling them what to do (Deak & Ackerley, 2017). Our **brain stem** controls things we don't think about, such as breathing, digestion, and pumping blood through our body. This is where our fight-flight-freeze response is located, and when we experience big emotions, we are not able to use the other parts of our brain well. Staying calm, learning, and working through problems become very difficult when we are operating in our fight-flight-freeze mode. Lots of different situations can trigger this, and trauma can create conditions where we are more easily triggered because of ongoing toxic stress. Just knowing these simple facts about the brain can help us understand what's happening when we experience big emotions. To learn more, watch the video *"Brain 101"* from National Geographic on YouTube.

TABLE 3.14 Link and QR code for "Brain 101"

Resource	Link to Access	QR Code to Access
Video: *"Brain 101"* from National Geographic	https://bit.ly/EASELbrain	

Use $10 emotion and feeling words. A key element of self-awareness is noticing our thoughts, feelings, and emotions. Everyone experiences a wide range of emotions and feelings on a daily basis, and increasing our awareness of the full range of emotions we experience helps us understand and work through them in a stronger way. Starting with four core emotions of happy, sad, mad and worried can help us with understanding the full range of emotions. I call those four base words "$1 words". I did some brainstorming to come up with more complex and subtle yet related emotions. I would call this list of more sophisticated emotion words "$10 words". They are less common, more complex in meaning, and more powerful than the base list.

TABLE 3.15 Emotions

Happy	Sad	Mad	Worried
Joy	Melancholy	Furious	Fear
Peaceful	Depressed	Spite	Anxious
Calm	Disappointed	Hatred	Jealous
Energetic	Hopeless	Irritated/Annoyed	Stuck
Exuberant	Confused	Triggered	Terrified
Ecstatic	Despondent	Angry	Unlucky
Buoyant	Glum	Bitter	Scared
Effervescent	Regret/Remorse	Agitated	Helpless

When we can more succinctly name what we are feeling, we are more likely to be able to deal with it. When we know more words and language around emotions, we can communicate what is happening to us in a better way. As a matter of habit now, when I am feeling an emotion, particularly annoyance, I task myself with drilling down to identify what I am truly feeling, so I can understand the trigger or root cause of the feeling. Once I do this, I am better able to face and handle the feeling and feel more equipped to talk to people directly about the feeling and do something about it.

I use this concept in a writing lesson with my students each year. We identify several $1 words such as good, bad, big, small, nice, and happy. Then I provide students with a list they can refer to all year to edit their writing to make it more powerful. They learn to use words such as fantastic, terrible, enormous, tiny, lovely, and ecstatic. Not only does this help them grow into more capable writers, it helps grow their verbal language skills in class; they can express ideas and feelings more succinctly and powerfully with more advanced words. It's a win on every level.

Feel deeply and honestly. When we experience emotions, various chemicals are released in our brains and they cause physical responses in the body. The stress chemical cortisol signals danger and, when released in high-enough levels, can initiate a fight-flight-freeze response when danger presents itself. Similarly, positive emotion chemicals, including serotonin, dopamine, endorphins, and oxytocin, are released when pleasure centers are activated.

After brainstorming a list of sophisticated emotion words, go back and identify how you feel when you experience them. These could be physical changes in the body or more in-depth descriptions of thoughts. Do this honestly. Close your eyes and visualize yourself going through these emotions to really access detailed feelings, descriptions, and ideas about what is happening in your body. You can see the results of my work in Figure 3.15. I added to the emotion and feeling brainstorm activity. My body words and thought descriptions are in italics below each emotion. These words explain how my physical body feels with the emotion, and knowing and understanding this will help me determine exactly what I am feeling in the moment. We can look for patterns in our feelings and body and this can enable us to recognize signs of emotions and then be better prepared to handle them.

Knowing the signs and deep feelings that signal a big emotion is coming will help us be alerted to the change. Armed with this very personal and individual data on our emotions, we can better navigate them as they arise. I'll talk more about specific strategies for this when we dive into self-management.

TABLE 3.16 Emotions and feelings

Happy	Sad	Mad	Worried
Joy *bright, light*	Melancholy *heavy*	Furious *teeth clench*	Fear *skin prickles*
Peaceful *still*	Depressed *can't move*	Spite *dark joy*	Anxious *sweaty*
Calm *ready*	Disappointed *frowning*	Hatred *shaking*	Jealous *shoulders sag*
Energetic *powerful energy*	Hopeless *empty inside*	Irritated/Annoyed *twitchy*	Stuck *heavy body*
Exuberant *electric*	Confused *eyes dart*	Triggered *tight inside, clumsy*	Terrified *on the start line*
Ecstatic *warm*	Despondent *immobile*	Angry *hot face*	Unlucky *cloudy thoughts*
Buoyant *bouncy*	Glum *cement feet*	Bitter *tight body*	Scared *nerves tingling*
Effervescent *walking on air*	Regret/Remorse *want to run*	Agitated *Itchy on inside*	Helpless *can't move*

Understand Your Mindset. What is a **mindset**?

Mindset is a key component of self-awareness. Our mental attitudes and inclinations impact what we do and say each day and over time.

TABLE 3.17 Definition of mindset

Mindset	A **mental** *attitude or* **inclination**

Being optimistic or pessimistic is nothing to be judged but rather critical information we can make use of. If we are pessimistic, we need to know this and how it impacts our daily lives. The same goes for optimism. How does an optimistic mindset impact our daily lives? We can also cultivate and work in a specific way toward a mindset we desire. I'll share some ways to do this in our chapter on self-management. For right now, let's embrace the idea that we just need to know where we are and our view of the world. Understanding the differences between optimism and pessimism can be helpful.

TABLE 3.18 Signs of optimism and pessimism

Signs of Optimism	Signs of Pessimism
You are hopeful about the future.	You think things will stay as they are.
You bounce back from defeat.	Setbacks are difficult to recover from.
You have a positive view of yourself and the world.	You focus on negative attributes of yourself, others, and the world.

This includes understanding whether or not we have a growth or fixed mindset. A growth mindset is one where we believe we can learn new things, grow from mistakes, and embrace challenges. It is a learner's mindset. With this, we're not afraid to try new things, we know it'll be messy along the way, and we understand that is OK. A fixed mindset is more rigid; it likes things the way they are. Since learning new things can be messy and uncomfortable, a fixed mindset is not open to new learning. When you determine what your mindset is, it's important not to judge it but rather just notice it, really notice it, so you know what you're capable of and where you are going. If you find yourself in a fixed mindset, that's good information. If that is the case, it might not be the time to tackle something new. Or that realization may spur the energy to change that through growth with a new experience. It's just key to know where you are. Where are you?

Understand Your Box of Energy

I love to embrace the idea that every day we wake up with a Box of Energy that we can take into our day. This Box of Energy can change size and look different each day and is influenced by multiple factors such as the amount of rest we get, the previous day's interactions and tasks, and the food we eat. It is also full of different things that can shapeshift and grow or shrink in size, depending what we've got on our plates. All of these various tasks and demands occupy space in our Box of Energy, so it's important to deeply understand them and think about all of them on a regular basis to foster self-awareness. This figure represents my thinking.

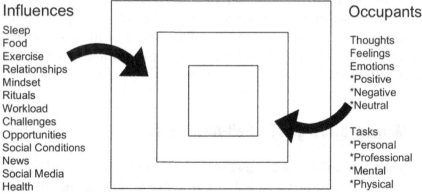

Figure 3.5 Understanding your Box of Energy.

When we are aware of what is influencing our energy on any given day, we can get better at predicting and preparing for days that are more challenging. The same goes for understanding when we may have days that are more relaxed and less stressful. On these days, we might be able to schedule conversations or tasks that are more demanding since we have room for them in our Box of Energy.

During a recent school year, I knew that my Box of Energy would be very full of tasks and negative thinking on Tuesdays, so I had to make sure it was as large as possible to get me through the day. This was because I had a tough schedule that day. My second graders had a special first thing in the morning, so the rest of the day was composed of long chunks of time without a break in the morning or the afternoon. I also had recess duty on that day, so after getting my students to lunch, checking my mailbox and using the restroom, I usually had about 20 minutes to eat, check email, and get ready for the rest of the day. In addition, we had staff meetings after school on Tuesday twice a month. So, on those tough days when my Box of Energy was very full of professional tasks, I tried to prepare well. I treated myself to coffee on the way to school. I made sure I went to bed at a decent time the night before. I optimized my morning routine and attended to it with fervor. It consists of mindful time in silence over coffee, setting my intentions and then exercising, all before I speak to anyone or look at technology. I also tried to make sure I drank enough water throughout the day and ate well so I could avoid any type of up and down or crash due to what I was eating and drinking. I check in with upbeat or positive friends on the way home. Then when I arrived home, I recovered. I would check in with my kids, and if nothing was urgent, I'd say "Please leave me alone for an hour". This didn't always work out, but by being self-aware in knowing I had more demands on me on Tuesday than any other day of the week, I could make sure that my Box of Energy was positively influenced in every way I could control.

There are so many strong and powerful proactive strategies we can embrace to increase our self-awareness. All of them have helped me become more of an expert on myself and increased my personal and professional success in relationships and with challenges and opportunities on a daily basis. Proactive self-awareness strategies are well worth the investment.

In-the-Moment Strategies for Self-Awareness

When confusion arises, ask questions. Ask Questions. And keep asking them. This simple strategy can help us find out what is going on with ourselves and others when we try to understand situations at hand. The very idea of an in-the-moment strategy for self-awareness is a difficult one. A lack of self-awareness means we are not informed. If we are not informed about a topic, we may not even consider it at the moment and it might not register on our radar.

For example, one year, I worked with a student who was away from our classroom for over a month. When they returned to class, they were completely overwhelmed and had a very difficult time functioning. Initially, we were all thrilled when this child returned to class, and when they entered the classroom on their first day back, students broke out in cheers and approached the student with hugs and enthusiastic greetings. Shortly after this arrival, the student went and stood in the corner. They didn't misbehave, act out, or cause a big problem, but they could not function. I became confused and realized I had no idea what was going on. As I became aware of my feelings of confusion, I noticed them without judgment, and I thought to act quickly to be responsive to the situation and meet my student's needs in this tough moment. So I started to ask questions to get more information. I asked:

- ★ Are you OK?
- ★ What do you need?
- ★ How can I help you right now?
- ★ What would be best right now?

I quickly realized the child was so overwhelmed they were having a hard time speaking. So I asked if they could write me a note. They nodded yes. In the note, they told me that they were scared and worried about coming back to school and that it was too loud. They asked me if they could work in the corner that first day. They also wanted to keep their hoodie up. Knowing that students who wear hoodies in school can be cold or stressed out, I heard and understood in our communication that this child was dealing with a great amount of stress and needed support. The behavior was important communication. Acknowledging my feeling of confusion and knowing that I didn't know where to go from there led me to using questions to increase my knowledge. It was my self-awareness of the feeling of confusion that led me there. This self-awareness opportunity happened organically, in the moment. When you need to, embrace a strategy of asking questions to help you through moments like this one.

When negative thoughts arise, reframe. Negative thoughts arise all the time. In fact, human beings have a negativity bias and we tend to pay attention to negative thoughts more than positive ones. Just think about it: On a busy day, when 9 out of 10 things go well, we dwell on the one thing that did not work out the way we wanted it to. Reframing is a practice where you can take a negative thought and see it in a different light, finding an opportunity or positive idea in it. At times, it can help us get to a positive place or at least to a neutral position on something. It is not being overly, toxically positive or seeing "rainbows and unicorns" in all parts of our life but rather a healthy way to change our thinking which can change the chemicals being released in our brains and help us feel better.

I use reframing thoughts as a way to find something positive or good in whatever is difficult. Reframing doesn't mean we diminish hard things or dismiss them. Instead, we look at them another way to see something as not quite so bad. For me right now, one of my difficulties is playing ping pong with our kids. We have two teenagers. They are both really good at ping pong, and I am terrible at it. Since I can be a fairly competitive person, it can be difficult for me to lose. It's like cooking. I am just not good at it and I know it. But it's still hard to accept and deal with sometimes. I have to work on my emotional regulation while I get crushed in the games regularly, sometimes mercilessly taunted by moody teenagers. So I keep playing to get better. I reframe the experience as time spent with my kids, active time, and access to my growth mindset around ping pong skills. In games now, I set a goal of scoring 5 points and having fun. I can do that! It's a win and I am getting better at both handling my emotions and playing the game.

In order to develop my reframing practice, I set specific goals for myself around reframing negative ideas, thoughts, and emotions. The first step was simply to notice my negative thoughts. Then, when I started to notice my negative thoughts, I'd commit to reframing one thought a day. When I did, I would make a mental note or record it in a note on my phone. When I had mastered that (it took about a week), I increased the goal to reframing once in the morning and once in the afternoon, again taking notes on my progress. A week after that practice was in place, I committed to using reframing at both home and at work. This meant I was intentionally reframing tough moments in my classroom. This made me feel so much better! I was building my resilience muscles as I worked in this practice. My final goal was to reframe at least four times a day: twice at home and twice at work. I am proud to say, it is now an automatic part of my practice. I support this practice by including it in my daily intention setting that is part of my morning routine. Here are some recent reframes I've made automatically.

Earlier this week, I came downstairs in the morning to a silent and quiet kitchen. I am usually the first one up, and I use this time for my mindful practice and to set my intention for the day before I look at technology or talk to anyone. On the kitchen table was a pile of nail clippings and the nail clipper. I wanted to scream and run away! Ew!! But I immediately reframed the situation. After we went to bed, our son, on his own and completely voluntarily, groomed himself without being asked. He even knew where to find the nail clippers! Even though this was a gross sight, it was a win and I had to reframe to see it that way. He received a friendly reminder to clean up after himself when he got up. I still smile to myself when I think about this one.

Similarly, I was greeted on another morning by an incredibly messy kitchen. There was dried-up batter on the floor and counters and all over the sink. Measuring cups, bowls, and a syrup bottle were out on the counter, and flour was everywhere! I looked closely and found the waffle iron in the middle of all of it with some eggshells nearby. Yep, you guessed it: our son had made homemade waffles after we went to bed and left the evidence everywhere. I could have easily slipped into annoyance and started slamming around cleaning everything up on my own and waking up the rest of the house to communicate my displeasure. But I took a deep breath and reframed. Our growing teenage son was hungry and fed himself. He made something from scratch. He knew where to find and how to use a cooking appliance and even had safely unplugged the waffle iron. Once again, he received a friendly reminder to clean up after himself and did so on his own before school. Are you noticing a trend here? I am. By reframing, I avoid conflict with our son, which helps to strengthen our relationship. He is forgetful and disorganized as his brain grows and develops but I am OK with that.

Reflective Strategies for Self-Awareness

Honest reflection challenges us to look deeply into a situation with the benefit of hindsight. With self-awareness, I embrace reflecting by identifying the root causes of emotions. This helps us to identify triggers and annoyances that we can later address proactively. Committing to this process should yield positive results that you can carry forward with you.

An example that occurred in my classroom a few years ago led me to fix a problem. We use a Positive Behavior Incentive Support (PBIS) system at our school. Students receive pride points (paper tickets) when they are meeting our behavior expectations: "The 3 To Be: Be Respectful, Be Responsible, Be Safe". I had created an area on a bulletin board where they could store their pride points by stapling small paper cups to the board that were labeled with each student's name. They would place the paper tickets in the cups throughout the day, and once a week students would count them. After music class one day, students arrived back in my classroom with pride points from the music teacher. When they entered the classroom, everyone charged over to the bulletin board to put away their tickets. It was a massive, unsafe mess. Students were pushing and shoving each other, the holders were being ripped off the bulletin board, and tempers started to flare. I was severely annoyed about the situation and disappointed in my students that they could not do this with self-control safely. Seven- and eight-year-olds can be impulsive and excited and forget to slow down and think, and this was one of those times.

That night, I reflected and realized I needed to fix the situation or create a limit that would help them meet expectations. So the next day, I repaired the board and put a piece of painter's tape about 10 feet away from the wall on the floor. I taught students that when they were putting away tickets, they should line up on the tape line and wait for the person in front of them to finish putting away their tickets before they put away their own. I showed them how to do this, they all practiced, and this new procedure became part of our classroom routine. Voilà! The problem was fixed, and it began with my process of self-reflection. This also led to a very powerful understanding for me: when things annoy me in my classroom, I need to fix them. If I let the problem linger and become part of our norms, that's on me. As the adult in the room, I have to guide growth and model problem-solving, even with very small situations. This is a great example of living this approach.

Tapping into my emotion of annoyance and back-mapping it to the root cause of the situation (my students' inability to manage themselves while putting away their pride points) allowed me to implement a quick and easy solution that eliminated the problem. If I had stayed in annoyance without any reflection, I most likely would not have been moved to solve the problem and would have complained about it each time it happened. My reflection led to problem-solving and the elimination of a situation where I might experience a negative emotion that could derail my day. Committing to this process has helped me to move forward from setbacks quickly and in a positive way that eliminates the same thing from happening again.

Personal Implications

Engaging in self-awareness practices helps us develop expertise in ourselves. What drives us, how we think, and why we do things the way we do and our culture, biases, strengths, and values all make us who we are. With deep self-awareness, we can discover ways to handle difficult moments and problems proactively. When we do this, we gain a sense of control and agency about who we are and how we live. The deep work and time required to do this are worth it! The rewards are many and will make life more enjoyable.

Since I have focused on this work, I have experienced a greater sense of enjoyment in my personal and professional life. I have stronger relationships and handle negativity and difficulty in better ways. I feel like I have control over what happens to me to a certain degree, and I am also able to teach my family, my students, and my co-workers some of these strategies, which benefits all of us. The incredible aspect of doing this work is that it benefits us as a whole human being and not just as a mom or teacher or neighbor; it helps us be more successful in all of our roles in life. If you embrace some of these practices, it's unlikely that you'll do them in only one context. They will become part of you that you'll take into your various roles and communities on a regular basis.

Professional Connection

Once you are comfortable with the self-awareness strategies shared here, bring them to your students and staff and your learning space as soon as possible. You will be able to model your work and authentically talk about how it feels to do this work, and you'll be an effective guide for others. Explicitly define self-awareness and come up with a plan to address all of the components.

Engaging in the work of self-awareness is like unlocking the mystery of ourselves. It's doing detective work on us. It's deep, fun, revealing, messy, and meaningful, and it's the start of your journey on the SEL Road to Success. As we build up our skills, we can see our progress. With this work, you are in the curiosity or competency zone on self-awareness and that is a great place to be.

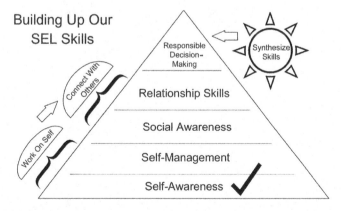

Figure 3.6 Building up our SEL skills.

Reflection Questions

It's time to reflect on and process the information we are learning. Feel free to go back into the chapter to dig into some of these ideas. You can answer these questions by thinking about them, recording ideas in a journal, adding notes here, or creating audio or video notes.

TABLE 3.19 Link and QR code for online reflection journal

\multicolumn{3}{l}{*I created an online tool with Google Jamboard that you can access and use on your own if you'd like to. You can access it below. When you access the file, you'll be asked if you want to make a copy of the file. Say "yes" and this file will be in your Google Drive for you to use and refer back to throughout your reading of the text.*}
Resource	**Bitly Link to Access**	**QR Code to Access**
"Embracing Adult SEL" Google Jamboard Reflection Journal	https://bit.ly/EASELjournal1-4	

TABLE 3.20 Reflection activity: Explain self-awareness with at least three ideas

Explain self-awareness. Share at least three ideas.		
Idea #1	**Idea #2**	**Idea #3**

TABLE 3.21 Reflection activity: Explain identity

Explain identity and create your own identity wheel. Use the template if you want to.
Identity is ...

TABLE 3.22 Reflection activity: Elements of culture

Describe surface, shallow, and deep culture. What are at least two components of your surface, shallow, and deep culture?			
Elements of Culture	**Surface**	**Shallow**	**Deep**
Describe it.			
Aspects of mine are			

TABLE 3.23 Reflection activity: Strengths

\: Name a few of your strengths and share how you use them in your daily life	
Strength	**How you use it**
1.	
2.	
3.	

TABLE 3.24 Reflection Activity: Emotions

\: Identify three emotions you experienced recently and how you felt when each was happening. This can be a physical body sensation or a deeper feeling.	
Emotion	**How You Felt**

TABLE 3.25 Reflection activity: The brain

Generally, explain how the brain works. Add a picture.
The brain ...

TABLE 3.26 Reflection activity: Implicit bias

Identify three blind spots you have related to implicit bias that you identified with three implicit bias tests for this question and explain how they could impact others.	
Blind Spot	**How It Could Impact Others**

TABLE 3.27 Reflection activity: Core values

Identify three core values and why they matter in your life.	
Core Value	**Why It Matters**

TABLE 3.28 Reflection activity: Reframing

Describe a recent situation from your personal or professional life and how you would reframe it.	
What happened?	**How could you reframe it?**

4

Managing Ourselves Matters
Learn, Practice, and Model Self-Management

I'll never forget the day when a red rubber bracelet was my most important accessory. After beginning our regular morning routine, I was confronted by an angry colleague in my classroom. We started to engage in a heated conversation—right in front of my students. I knew this was bad. I knew my students were watching, and I knew I had to get my social emotional house in order, fast!

After a couple of minutes, we ended the conversation, but the issues were unresolved. When I shut the door, I didn't go back to the morning meeting. I couldn't, not the way my emotions were at that moment. I simply could not teach. So I walked over to a small basket that holds red, green, and yellow rubber bracelets. We all put one on every morning to share how we are feeling without words. I took off the green one I was wearing and put on a red one, while 20 pairs of student eyes bored into my soul. I simply told my students I needed to cool down, then went over to our breathing bucket—or cool-down area—and breathed deeply for several minutes while they continued.

I was then able to return to my students and my job in a much more productive emotional state. I modeled EXACTLY what I would want them to do in the same situation. I later realized that this moment was an incredible gift, a chance to show my students how to handle difficult emotions when they arise unexpectedly. It was my opportunity to model self-awareness and practice adult social emotional learning (SEL).

I'll be honest. I was incredibly proud of how I handled myself that day in front of my students. It was a teachable moment. It was the curriculum of real life. It was not in the lesson plan, but we all know that some of the most incredible and valuable lessons are unscripted and unplanned, interrupting what we thought we would do. But we must see them, embrace them, and love them for what they are: valuable life lessons and a chance to model SEL authentically.

Each day in my classroom, we all put on small, colored rubber bracelets to share how we are feeling with our classroom community in a non-verbal way. I do this too. We use four colors: red, green, yellow, and blue. Green means "good" or "ready-to-go", yellow represents "so-so" or maybe something's not quite right or might be bothering us, red is "not OK", and blue is "sad" or "down". Students can change their bracelets throughout the day as needed, which is incredibly revealing and helps us all to connect in an even deeper way. The big picture message is "All emotions are OK; we just need to know what to do when big ones come up". Before we use these bracelets, I teach my students how the brain works and what happens when they encounter challenging emotions. They know and understand what the "amygdala" is and that it's our emotional center. This learning about the brain is essential to our classroom culture and the use of bracelets. Here are some pictures of the bracelets as well as an emotion poster from our classroom.

Figure 4.1 Rubber bracelets in the classroom.

Managing Ourselves Matters ◆ 79

Figure 4.2 Emotion check-in with rubber bracelets.

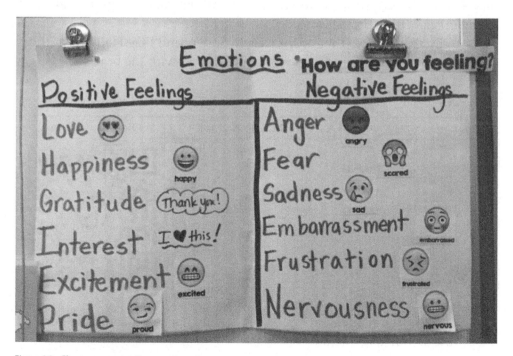

Figure 4.3 Classroom emotion poster.

This poster is the original version I initially created for use in my classroom. It looks slightly different now. One day as we were discussing emotions, one of my brilliant students raised his hand and said "Mrs. Turner, sadness is not a negative emotion". Again, I was stopped cold in my tracks by this powerful statement, so I had to really stop and pay attention. I asked the student to tell us more. He said sadness just happens and it's not bad; it just makes you sad for a while and then it goes away. My brilliant student! I changed the heading on the right to read "Difficult Emotions". I think if I were to remake the poster now, the headings may read "Comfortable" and "Uncomfortable" emotions. I love listening to and learning from my students.

To be clear, I didn't invent this idea. I learned about it in a breakout session at the Delaware Annual Policy and Practice Institute in June 2017 while I was the Teacher of the Year. The presenter was sharing trauma-informed strategies and mentioned a teacher who used "those little rubber bracelets" to see how kids are feeling. I had no idea who the teacher was or what they taught, the subject matter content, the age of the students, or even the details of how the bracelets were used, but it didn't matter. I was completely intrigued. So I started to think about this and how I could use a system like this in my classroom and came up with a plan for the next school year. One of my strengths is that when I learn about something that sounds like it could work in my classroom, or my life, I'll immediately try it. My growth mindset kicked in the moment I heard about this, and I just went for it with great success. For years now, small, colored rubber bracelets have helped us all with self-management in the classroom.

You can read a piece I wrote for Kristin Souers and Pete Hall, the authors of *Fostering Resilient Learners*, on how to get started with the bracelets.

TABLE 4.1 Link and QR code for "Rubber Bracelets to Support Emotional Regulation? Absolutely!"

Resource	Link to Access	QR Code to Access
Blog: "*Rubber Bracelets to Support Emotional Regulation? Absolutely!*"	https://bit.ly/FRL Bracelets	

What is self-management? Let's once again construct some meaning of the phrase self-management.

TABLE 4.2 Definitions of self and management

Self	*An* **individual's** *typical* **character** *or* **behavior**
Management	*The* **conducting** *or* **supervising** *of something*

With these definitions, we can start to understand that self-management is related to conducting or supervising our individual self.

Self-management is all about being able to manage ourselves as we live our lives, both personally and professionally, while experiencing feelings and emotions during opportunities and challenges. It happens all day, every day. We can be with people we know well or strangers when we do it. We can be alone. It's how "you do you". It can be easy to manage ourselves or extraordinarily difficult or outright demanding, depending on the situation. One aspect of self-management is that it's constant; it's always required. That means we need to do it on our best days, our worst days, our most exhausted or frustrating days, and our dream days. Because this quality is so critical and ubiquitous in our lives, it makes a lot of sense to build and practice our self-management skills on a regular basis and then model them authentically for kids.

Casel defines self-management as "the abilities to manage one's emotions, thoughts, and behaviors effectively in different situations and to achieve goals and aspirations. This includes the capacities to delay gratification, manage stress, and feel motivation and agency to accomplish personal and collective goals." It includes "identifying and using stress management strategies, exhibiting self-discipline and self-motivation, setting personal and collective goals, using planning and organizational skills, showing the courage to take initiative and demonstrating personal and collective agency." It's many ideas rolled into one critical skill that children and adults need in order to live their lives and thrive.

Self-management helps us think deeply about how we handle stress, what we do when we experience feelings and emotions, as well as how to motivate ourselves as we learn, set goals, and strive to move forward. My approach in coming up with proactive strategies is centered on the idea of being efficient. We all have so much energy we can access at the beginning of each day. Each day is a new opportunity to manage ourselves in a way that makes sense. Some days this will be a heavy load; other days may breeze by without the intense need for self-management. We need to be prepared for all of them! We are multi-faceted human beings with myriad experiences and complexities. When we work to build our skills to foster calm and positive emotions and the ability to work through challenging ones, we are prepared and competent at self-management. Successfully managing intense anger or extreme sadness is as powerful and important as fostering calm and cultivating happiness.

It makes sense to explore strategies to support our self-management. With this work, we are once again in the Confidence Zone of SEL, understanding how to engage in strategies that support our skill development and live in SEL.

Proactive Strategies for Self-Management

Foster calm at key times. I became a mother a week before I turned 35 years old. This was much older than my mom was when she had me, her first child, at 22. For my generation, this is not unusual or out of the ordinary, and it was truly transformational for me in the very best of ways. But it was hard. I had traveled for my jobs in the business world when I was younger, lived in cities, and enjoyed lots of adventures with family and friends. I loved settling down and getting married and looked forward to having a family. I was completely thrilled to become a mom, and in a span of just 20 months, I was taking care of two kids in diapers and working. I chose to work and knew it was the right way for me. It was wonderful but it was a lot. I knew I had to figure out how to pour into myself so I could do everything I needed to do, meeting my family's needs and hopefully not losing my mind. My answer was and still is the morning calm.

For as long as I can remember, I have been getting up before everyone else in the house whenever possible. Everyone. This was a challenge when our kids were learning how to sleep through the night, but once we got through that stage, I had a choice about when to get up: before, with, or after others. I chose to get up before others. This means I swap sleep for time for myself and this works well for me. Of course, it won't work well for everyone else. I have lots of flow and energy in the morning, so this makes sense for me. But for many others, lunch time, evening or late at night, or time spent on a commute or walking the dog may be the key time. The important thing is to think intentionally about this and find your key time.

During my morning calm, I follow a routine every day. My routine is getting up, feeding and letting out the dog, and making myself a cup of coffee. I then sit quietly and enjoy every sip of the coffee. I notice the smell of the coffee, I love that smell, so I really enjoy it fully and take it in. Then I feel the warmth of the mug on my hands, even on a hot summer day, and think about the day ahead. I like to hold the mug with both hands fully around it, almost in a hug, so I can absorb that feeling in a significant way. During warm weather, I do this on our back porch, and in cooler times, it's in the living room. I don't touch a phone or a computer during this time. In my mind, I am setting my intentions. I say to myself things like "Today I will have a positive outlook and look for the best in all situations". I also say things like "I will be kind to my family, students, and co-workers". Some days I say "Today is going to be very hard, I have to do my best to stay calm, preserve my energy, and work every hour well until the end of a long day" or "Today is REALLY important due to a big opportunity, I need to stay calm, cool and organized to make the most of it". I might think of a friend or two to text a quick check-in or funny picture or motivational quote. If I know there are certain challenges ahead in the day such as a tough meeting, recess duty, or dentist appointment, I think about these as well. If I am outside, I listen for birds and wind or notice squirrels and rabbits in the yard as it gets light out. This takes a good 15 minutes and is my way of being mindful. I don't practice formal meditation, but if I did this is mostly like when it would happen. This is my own, personal, mindful moment.

I make a second cup of coffee. Can you tell I love coffee? On work days, I drink it when I get dressed and when I get ready to exercise. Some days this involves a car ride to the local YMCA, and some days it's on an exercise bike at home. Before I go, I look at my phone to see what emails await me and quickly scan social media. But I purposely avoid engaging in communication and problem-solving or replying to emails until later in the day. On the weekends, I read while I enjoy that second cup of coffee. It's always a book vs. an article or blog I can pull up on the phone. For some reason, there is something comforting to me in holding a book and physically turning the pages. I usually switch back and forth between fiction and non-fiction titles. Again, this works well for me. It's important to identify and find what works well for you. You might enjoy playing an online game or doing a puzzle or watching your favorite show. There are no rules about this, no way to fail at it. We just need to think deeply about ourselves, think about what will help create that calm, and make a plan to do it.

Another key time of the day for me is lunch time. I came to realize over the years that I needed that time to myself to experience some quiet after the morning in the classroom with my students before the demands of the afternoon ahead. I put on some quiet music in my classroom and eat lunch quickly and quietly, thinking about what I need to do to get ready for the afternoon. I explain to my colleagues that I don't mean to be anti-social by not eating lunch with anyone but that I need the time to restore myself. Our school has a quarter-mile walking track around the recess area. When I can, I walk my students to lunch and walk right outside to walk around that track one time before I come back in for lunch. When we were required to wear masks to school during Covid, I sat outside to eat, even when it was cold out, just to get some fresh air and to be able to take a breath. Lunch has always been a key time for me and I used it wisely to restore myself so I can feel and be better for my students in the afternoon.

The end of the school day is also a critical moment for me. The demands of working with and serving students all day tend to leave me feeling exhausted at 4 p.m. I remember when I was a student teacher at age 39, after my full days in a first-grade classroom, I would come home and collapse on the couch! I couldn't believe how much energy we needed to get through the day. I am used to the pace and cadence of a school day now, but I am honest with myself in acknowledging that it takes a toll. Because of this, I use my commute home to unwind, often not even turning on any music or a podcast, opening the windows if I could to "just be" on my way home. On this ride, I leave behind whatever went wrong and just move forward into the rest of the day. I knew I wanted to be present and available for my family and that I may need to do some school work as well. The quiet ride on the way home is critical for me, especially if I have to go right to another activity or meet another demand right away.

I have lots of friends who are night owls and love the quiet time after others in their homes go to bed. Some people are just not morning people no matter what they do. The beauty of this idea is that it can work for you no matter what your key time of the day or night is.

To create calm at key moments, I recommend doing the following:

1. Identify your key time(s) of day:
   a. Name this time or times.
   b. Identify where you will be.
2. Create a plan for your key time, identifying these details:
   a. How long it will last
   b. What you will do as your routine
   c. Write it out or record a voice note so you can look back at your plan and revise it if necessary
3. Reflect on your practice.
   a. Try it for one week.
   b. Notice your thoughts and feelings while you do it.
   c. Name how your practice affects you at other times of the day.

I've found that I'm better able to stay calm and meet challenges when I name them earlier in the day during my quiet, mindful intention-setting. I also notice that when I don't have my time in the morning to create a sense of calm and go through my routine, I feel the difference. I am more edgy and can be more easily triggered when I am not able to engage in this routine. It is a clear and powerful difference for me! Therefore, I will protect this morning time fiercely. It is quite simply a necessary part of my practice as a human and a key proactive self-management strategy. One of my most important tools in this practice is my alarm clock. I check it every night before bed. I leave my phone in another room while I sleep so I'm not tempted to pick it up and I don't have notifications interrupting my sleep.

Practice kindness. What exactly does kind mean?

TABLE 4.3 Definition of kind

Kind	Of a sympathetic or **helpful** nature

A focus on the word helpful reminds us how being kind impacts the receiver. Someone we show kindness to will receive the benefit of the help whether it's in the form of being assisted with a task, an emotional connection, a generosity, or helping words. As we engage in acts of kindness, we can feel better. When we feel better, we'll be able to manage ourselves more easily. Positive emotions are much easier for me to manage both personally and professionally. When they appear, I can notice and enjoy them. When difficult emotions arise, I need to notice and then intentionally manage them. This takes focus and energy and can make meeting challenges and completing everyday tasks more difficult. Managing challenging emotions occupies space in my Box of Energy. This can also effectively shrink my Box of Energy if it detracts from practices that help me build it up.

According to the Greater Good Magazine, which provides "science-based insights for a meaningful life", practicing kindness can make us happier and healthier. I do not think, by any means, that kindness will solve our biggest problems and fix injustices or enormous challenges in the world. I want to be clear on this. But I do think there is value in practicing kindness in our everyday lives, and, I'll be honest, I feel good when I am kind! Practicing kindness can create and keep positive emotions flowing and will help with our self-management. We can do this with people we know, strangers, our students, immediate and extended family members, and those in our communities.

Empatico, an online platform that connects classrooms around the world to building connection, understanding, and empathy, shares three ways to be kind.

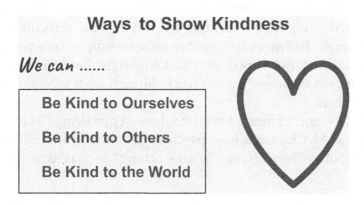

Figure 4.4 Three ways to show kindness.

I love the simplicity and power of this idea! It is a concrete way to understand kindness more deeply than just "being nice". I explain to my students that being kind is different from being nice. Being kind is going out of your way to do something that you don't have to. It's intentional and can be unexpected. With three ways to do it, we have options around how we can practice kindness. With any skill that we are building, we can embrace an approach that provides a roadmap. Thinking about kindness this way is helpful and can ignite creativity and purpose. If we flip our thinking about kindness and embrace it in the context of what it can do for us first, it may help us prioritize acts of kindness. Thinking about different ways to be kind increases the volume of kind acts we can show and may increase the benefits we experience.

A study cited by *The New York Times* in their article "The Other Side of Languishing Is Flourishing. Here's How to Get There" indicated that college students who practiced five acts of kindness in a single day "experienced more significant increases in well-being than those who spread out five kind things over the course of a week". So, even though all of the study participants were engaging in acts of kindness, the clustering of kindness increased the benefit. Focusing on multiple acts of kindness in our practices may increase our own wellness.

I think about kindness during my morning calm in my intention setting. It's lovely to consider what small things I can do during the day that will be helpful to those around me and generate personal wellness. I started working on kindness during the pandemic, doing kind deeds for my family when we were all stuck at home. This was anything from refilling someone's water bottle to delivering a small snack during a lengthy zoom session to plugging in someone's device when they forgot to charge it. I was kind to myself by taking a walk around the block between my students' morning and afternoon zoom sessions, sitting on the front steps to take in a bit of sun when I could, or playing fetch with our dog outside. We can practice kindness in our communities by volunteering, embracing environmental stewardship, and modeling the practice. It's hard to do this when things are difficult and we are working through challenges because we feel a weight on us when the world and life are not kind. But armed with the knowledge that practicing kindness supports our own wellness, we can work through what we are facing while supporting others.

Practice "3 Good Things". I first heard about practicing "3 Good Things" from Dr. Byron McClure, a school psychologist, author, and SEL expert. He shared this tool for identifying "What's Strong" vs. "What's Wrong" in a webinar I attended in the spring of 2020 at a time when we all needed help and practical strategies to focus on the positive aspects of our lives. Once again, I was immediately captivated by a simple approach that was easy to do and could help increase our wellness. I wanted to try it right away.

The practice of "3 Good Things" is about identifying and really seeing what's going well vs. what is wrong. At the time, I really needed this. The lockdown and school closure were taking a toll on me. Our children were in seventh and ninth grade, and you could really sense and see their struggle as they were not able to spend time with friends, had to attend zoom school, and started staying up until all hours of the night in an attempt to have some control over their lives. Personally, my worry increased dramatically, and it was a struggle to stay present in the moment and focus on what I could control instead of worrying about what might happen. This practice is not about ignoring what is tough or not going well but about choosing to highlight aspects and moments of our lives that are positive in the name of generating enjoyable emotions and feelings.

We started using this approach at home. A few times a week at dinner, we would go around the room and everyone would share three good things about their day. These aspects of our lives could be so small, microscopic even, but they were there! We found them and we said them out loud. All of us. Even our teenagers! It immediately changed the air in the room and brought smiles. It could be as simple as the sun was out, we got to walk the dog, we texted a friend, or we didn't burn the toast. Nothing was off limits. As a family, we still use this practice today, years later. At times, one of our teenage children will even suggest it. This is one of my 3 Good Things, that people in my life are internalizing and using a strategy that is good for them.

In the following school year, I started using this practice in class. I modeled it for my students during the first week of school and it became one of our optimistic closing routines that we used each week. My students were also able to identify and share what was good. We did this online with Google Jamboard so students at home and in school could all participate and see what others were bringing into the space. With the return to the classroom the next year, we enjoyed this positive closing ritual with an in person closing circle. Like reframing negative thoughts, 3 Good Things is now a part of my life; it happens automatically on a regular basis. It's one of the very good things I do to help me stay regulated and proactively contributes to my ability to manage myself.

You can read a blog I wrote here on using 3 Good Things as a positive practice for educators.

TABLE 4.4 Link and QR code for "3 Good Things, Positive Practices for Educators"

Resource	Link to Access	QR Code to Access
Blog: "*3 Good Things, Positive Practices for Educators*"	https://bit.ly/EASEL3good	

Embrace nature. Research indicates that spending time outside is linked to improved well-being. In *Nurtured by Nature*, Kirsten Weir writes:

> "From a stroll through a city park to a day spent hiking in the wilderness, exposure to nature has been linked to a host of benefits, including improved attention, lower stress, better mood, reduced risk of psychiatric disorders and even upticks in empathy and cooperation."

Before the pandemic, I didn't think about going outside with intention. It was something I did in good weather more often than in bad conditions. We spent time outdoors when our kids were young as we explored playgrounds, enjoyed seasonal festivals, and visited beaches when we could. I have always loved to run outside in warm weather and enjoy walking as well. Enjoying a barbeque or a firepit was a part of life that happened on a regular basis. But we never scheduled it, it just happened. I also never connected it with wellness.

Life in the pandemic was so different. Everything changed all at once, and our stress and anxiety levels were much higher than they used to be. As we were living with this, I started to think about how we could intentionally feel better with easy-to-implement practices. Going outside became part of my daily routine during lockdown, zoom teaching, and post-pandemic teaching at school. I found I needed more ways to invest in wellness and feeling better, which would then make it easier for me to manage myself with my students, friends, and family.

I take a walk around our walking path at school once a day whenever I can. It's 5 minutes for me and I feel better when I can do it. If that's too much, I can walk out the side door of our school and then around to the front and that's a few minutes of fresh air and open spaces. Movement also benefits us by creating brain activity that is not present when we are still. Going outside and moving is an efficient way to foster self-management.

Even looking at images of nature can yield positive results. I found this out firsthand when I was teaching second grade on zoom in 2021. I had noticed that student energy levels varied widely, and I wanted to figure out how to do something about it while we were learning online. This was a huge challenge! One January weekend, I came across an online photo collection of winter scenes in Scandinavia; they were stunning, ranging from reindeer to icy snowscapes, Northern Lights, and winter bonfires. The next Monday, I did an emotion check-in with my students and found that many were tired or bored at the beginning of our day. They shared this by indicating their emotional state on Google Jamboard slide. Then I showed 15 different pictures of the gorgeous Nordic winter scenes for 30 seconds each. At the conclusion of the slideshow, I did another emotion check-in. The emotion of calm was expressed in more students by a factor of 5. In other words, five times as many students felt calm after they viewed the pictures! I was shocked and excited to see the power of the nature scenes. From that moment on, I began to regularly incorporate scenes of nature into my classroom environment. I did this when students arrived, before we took a quiz, or when it just seemed the group would benefit from calm. There are lots of incredible resources available online, including bird feeder cams, aquarium timers, or aerial photography of beautiful places on earth.

As nature scenes and sounds foster calm feelings, this creates a mental state that is easier to manage than one filled with more difficult feelings and emotions. This proactive practice is another way to help us invest in self-management so we can better manage ourselves.

Take brain breaks. Ding. It's my watch going off again, reminding me it's time to stand. What used to be annoying is a helpful reminder to take a break. As I have learned about and embraced brain breaks as a positive practice that supports self-management, I can see the benefits in many other aspects of my life.

As I write this book, I am sitting at a desk for long periods of time, working to put the words on paper. I am conscious of family members coming home at certain times later in the day, knowing that there will be demands made for me to be physically and emotionally present. I feel knots in my shoulders. I have two options:

a. I can write all day, stopping quickly to gobble down food in the name of productivity right up until the moment another family member gets home or needs me to do something. In this scenario,

I may be quick to anger or annoyance given my lack of movement and the long hours of pressure to perform. An unsuspecting family member may come to me with a reasonable, everyday request or even just say hello and it could set me off, confusing the person involved and creating the need for repair later on. Repeated instances like this can damage my relationships.

OR

b. I can take a small break of 5 to 10 minutes every hour or two to help me stay regulated. This will foster more calm and pleasant emotions instead of difficult emotions that I have to spend precious energy managing. I will most definitely write fewer words, but I will be in a better place to support others in my life and will feel better if I can avoid stress. This may actually support more productivity later on.

Brain breaks are a simple, wise, efficient, and free investment in our self-management and can be part of our proactive daily practice that supports calm brains. When we use them, it can help us stay away from bigger and more complicated emotions that we have to spend more energy managing. It's a "no-brainer" for me.

Develop a growth mindset. I had one particularly powerful moment as a mom that helped me authentically understand the growth mindset. The first time it revealed itself to me was when my daughter was 12. Each morning before school, she would ask me to braid her hair. And I was terrible at it, completely awful. I would usually rush through the process because of the stress of weekday mornings and the fact that I knew I wasn't very good at it, similar to cooking. It immediately triggered me! I didn't divide her hair evenly, the braids were lumpy, the end product was far from superior and some days was barely acceptable, and we both knew it. My daughter often asked me to redo the braids; I complied as needed, in defeat, but my second effort was no better than the first. Some days she simply sighed and said, "Thanks Mom, I think I'm just going to wear my hair down today." She said it kindly and added, "I know you are doing the best you can." She then spoke wistfully about her friends wearing French braids, Dutch braids, small braids on the sides of their head, Princess Leia braids, crowns of braids, and the moms and sisters of girls with braiding superpowers. I was crushed inside, but we moved on. I felt the failure and resolved to get better: to watch how-to videos on YouTube, to practice on a doll, to practice on my daughter at night, whatever it took! But my stomach remained knotted with self-doubt. I am an award-winning teacher, I have run seven half marathons, and I can't braid my daughter's hair the way she wants me to. I would take a deep breath and then say, "I am sorry hon, I am just not there YET."

YET is the most critical word we need to use when we think and talk about growth mindset. Carol Dweck says,

> "In a growth mindset students understand that their talents and abilities can be developed through effort, good teaching, and persistence. They don't necessarily think everyone's the same or anyone can be Einstein, but they believe everyone can get smarter if they work at it."

If you agree with this thinking, it is perfectly alright not to be there YET. We can get there; it takes hard work, effort, the proper mindset, and celebration of failure, but we can do it. A question stuck with me; how do I intentionally embrace and foster my own growth mindset?

I have been working tirelessly to answer this question. In my heart, I know that embracing and embodying a growth mindset are critical for successful human beings. I am fortunate to have a growth mindset! How do I know this? My most powerful growth mindset moment occurred that day in my cubicle when I called my husband and told him I wanted to be a teacher. At that moment, if I hadn't believed that I could attend school at night while working full-time for years, learn a completely new skill, and eventually be successful at it while taking care of young children, I never would have asked. This was long before I had heard of growth mindset, but it was there. It simply needed to be awoken with a new challenge. Since then, I have used my growth mindset to reach many goals, both personal and professional. I achieved a challenging personal best when running a half marathon after years of work, training, and coaching. I helped my elementary school achieve the status of "Green Ribbon School" with the US Department of Education through years of work building consensus, funding, and programming, and the relationships necessary to do so. I could never have completed any of these missions without the belief that I could do so and without the understanding of the steps that needed to occur in order to climb the mountain and reach the summit.

As part of your journey, look for growth. Call it out and name it in no uncertain terms. This is working well for us as a family on several levels right now. Our son Mike made the varsity wrestling team in his sophomore year of high school. This was unexpected and he was thrilled but quickly realized he was the weakest and most inexperienced member of the team. In early season matches, he was often pinned in the first period. But he got better. He had outstanding coaches who pushed him to develop his skills, spent time with him reviewing his matches, held him to an incredibly high standard of excellence, and continually told him that he was an important part of the team. Over time, he improved significantly. The last two matches of the season he lost, like every single one before them. But the difference was that he was not getting pinned, and he was going the distance in the matches, lasting all three periods. He lost his final match in the state championship dual by just one point. He grew enormously and his acceptance of struggle and working through it grew his grit and resilience tremendously. Doing so helped him learn how to manage himself in defeat and disappointment better. He simply became more skilled at it and changed his thinking: instead of failures, they were learning moments or "first attempts in learning". He was growing forward.

Like me in the kitchen with my daughter and the task of braiding, or our son on the wrestling mat, what is your growth mindset moment? I am sure you have one! Take the time to think about when you learned a new skill or overcame a challenge. We have all done it. Even if a growth mindset is not something you think about often or is central to your being, it's something that we can all understand in the context of a growth experience we have had. Uncover that experience! The very act of me writing this book is steeped in growth mindset, and while it's incredibly challenging, it's pushing me in ways that are new and that will result in some wonderful growth for me.

Prioritize sleep. Thinking about sleep was not something I had done a lot in my life. I always felt like sleep is just something we all do; it happens every day and sometimes it's good (satisfying, sound, and refreshing) and other times it's just not, particularly after a restless night spent tossing and turning or sweating, fighting a busy brain that won't turn off, or dealing with the dreaded Sunday night teacher jitters that just come with the job. Sleep could elude me during storms or when waking to take care of a hungry baby. I didn't really approach it with any intentional thought. But one thing was very clear to me. How I slept impacted many other parts of my life: how I could do my job, my relationships, and my mental well-being. It was similar to my thinking about going outside; both were something I did every day, but I never gave deep thought to either practice. This changed for me after I did some learning.

A local friend of ours who also happens to be a doctor ran a wellness challenge earlier this year. My husband and I signed up to participate. We had some health goals in mind but wanted to learn more. Week 3 was all about the power of sleep. Dr. David Donohue shared that insufficient sleep can cause many problems, including the common complaints of fatigue, low energy, moodiness, and irritability. These words hit me like a freight train. When my Box of Energy is small or full, I am moody and irritable and that makes it very difficult to be a good mom, wife, friend, or teacher.

I was delighted to learn that focusing on sleep could help, but I had to really think about it with intention to create a positive shift. Then I needed to know exactly how to do it. Dr. Dave's advice is to follow these practices for optimal sleep.

TABLE 4.5 Recommendations for quality sleep

Recommendations for Quality Sleep from Dr. David Donohue
1. Sleep and wake up at the same time every day.
2. Get outside for sunlight on awakening.
3. Exercise daily, especially outside.
4. Starchy breakfast for energy. Hydrate in the afternoon. Low salt at night.
5. Avoid caffeine and chocolate after 12 noon.
6. Reduce or avoid alcohol.
7. Avoid food within three hours of bedtime or in the middle of the night.
8. When the sun goes down, begin to turn off and dim lights.
9. Avoid artificial light of all kinds at least one hour before bed (screens).
10. Install light-blocking window blinds in your bedroom.
11. Keep your bedroom at a cool 65-67 degrees.
12. Set your bedtime to give yourself a sleep opportunity of at least eight hours.
13. Have the same bedtime and waking time each day.
14. Sleep mask and ear plugs can be beneficial.
15. Don't lie awake. Read, stretch, or meditate. Return to bed when sleepy.

When I looked at this list, I was both immediately excited and instantly intimidated. I knew that some of these practices would be very hard for me and, on some days, impossible to do successfully. I love to have a cup of coffee in the afternoon; it is part of my daily unwinding and recovery process, and I truly enjoy it, so it's unlikely that I would eliminate caffeine after 12 noon. I noticed that without judgment and looked for other entry points for me into some new practices around sleep. Upon reflection, I committed to trying just three things from the list. This way I could work to find some success without feeling like a failure. By embracing a growth mindset and working to build new habits around sleep, I could start small and celebrate growth and success. I focused on buying better shades, sleeping and waking at the same time as much as possible, and keeping the bedroom temperature cool. These things were all within my reach and could help me get started. With an eye toward self-management, practices that foster successful sleep can leave us less irritable and moody. With that shift, we'll have to spend energy managing negative emotions less often. This can help us be more successful in our lives.

Stay out of judgment. Judgment. It can be so satisfying. What is it exactly?

TABLE 4.6 Definition of judgment

Judgment	The process of **forming an opinion** or evaluation by discerning and **comparing**

Forming an opinion is activating our personal belief system. It takes energy. We do it all the time. As humans, we all have our own moral compass, deeply held beliefs, and culture, as explored in the previous chapter. When we judge, we compare our opinions and the related actions and behaviors with the beliefs, behaviors, and actions of others. When we sit in a place of judgment, we may think that our beliefs are better than someone else's or that their behaviors and actions are less than ours. We view their beliefs and choices as inferior. Again, it takes energy to do this. This is a key point to consider in the context of our Box of Energy.

The most powerful definition of mindfulness I have ever heard was shared by Dr. Jim Walsh, a Delaware-based clinical therapist specializing in pastoral counseling, at a mindfulness session he led at our school. He explained that to be mindful is "to notice without judgment". I was stopped cold in my tracks by this simple yet powerful idea. Like so many others, I had long confused mindfulness with meditation. Meditation is a way to achieve mindfulness and is a proven and powerful practice for many. But not for me. I find meditation to be too slow for me, I often doze off when attempting to do it (I better work on my sleep), and I feel edgy in the stillness of it. All of this probably indicates that I SHOULD embrace meditation. But as I have explained, I've got my own ways of being mindful with my calm morning practice, quiet car rides home, time in nature, and being still at key times of the day.

Dr. Walsh's words speak to me in a powerful way about judgment. Judgment is analysis of other's words and actions and then the application of an opinion about them. The very act of judging requires enormous amounts of energy, and the very nature of it can produce negative feelings. Of course, we can judge someone as good, moral, fair, or admirable, but since we are hard-wired to notice negative thoughts and feelings more readily than positive ones, our judgment may also default to that which is more negative. So I simply work to avoid it as much as possible. Upon reflection, I have come to believe the following:

★ Being judgmental about someone or something doesn't help me or make me feel authentically good.
★ Applying judgment to someone or something takes time, energy, and effort.
★ In my daily efforts to be self-aware and to manage myself, I need every ounce of energy and strength I can muster for the process.
★ Judgment takes energy and therefore reduces my personal capacity to be self-aware and manage myself.
★ To maximize the energy I have for self-awareness and self-management, I will stay out of judgment as much as possible.

I have come to the conclusion that judging others is a waste of my time and energy. It doesn't make me feel good, it doesn't help situations, and it is an inefficient use of my precious resources that I need to manage myself and get through my day. Avoiding judgment has become another way I invest in my self-management.

With a menu of self-management strategies, we can learn about, consider, and choose and embrace what is best for us. We can proactively grow our own ability to manage ourselves. The goal is never to eliminate or look down on the occurrence of difficult and complex emotions but rather create practices and ways to help us manage ourselves and stay regulated so we can enjoy and be successful in the various aspects of our lives.

In-the-Moment Strategies for Self-Management

Despite our best efforts, proactive practices, and commitments to strong self-management, we'll all encounter moments where we need to handle tough and complex emotions in the moment. That's just the way it goes with being human. Some of them may be predictable, such as when a known trigger surfaces in an everyday situation, while others may spring up out of nowhere and suddenly challenge us. Whatever the case, it makes sense to have some "go-to", in-the-moment strategies to help us navigate these moments.

Use affective statements. I first learned about affective statements when our school staff was going through training in restorative practices. Our trainer was the inspirational Dr. Malik Muhammad. I had heard him speak at the Delaware Trauma Symposium earlier that year. He delivered a powerful breakout session on the collective power to heal, sharing his personal journey in the process.

We were extraordinarily fortunate to work with Dr. Muhammad. His book *The Restorative Journey* served as our guide. In the section on practice, Dr. Muhammad writes:

"We refer to the ability to express the full range of emotion verbally as 'wielding affective language'. That is, it is the ability to communicate verbally when we are sad, frustrated, overjoyed, ashamed, and fascinated. It requires us not just to have a wide vocabulary at our disposal, but also to have the ability to connect this emotional vocabulary to our own internal experience of feelings and emotions. Just like the development of any language, affective language is taught, encouraged and refined".

(Muhammad, 2019, p. 90)

I'll add "practiced" to this list. "Affective statements are 'I' statements that express emotion and are connected to behavior" (Muhammad, 2019, p. 91).

To enhance our understanding of this concept, let's look at the meaning of these two words themselves.

TABLE 4.7 Definition of affective and statement

Affective	**Relating to,** *arising from, or influencing* **feelings** *or* **emotions**
Statement	*A single* **declaration** *or* **remark**

Given these definitions, we can understand that an affective statement is a remark or declaration about a feeling or emotion. Dr. Muhammad connects these statements to a behavior. In the context of Adult SEL, Dr. Muhammad writes: "We teach affective language through both modeling and explicit instruction" (Muhammad, 2019, p. 90). Once again, I was stopped cold in my tracks. Affective statements could help me to process and share my emotions and feelings, and I could model this authentically for my students.

I made plans to start using affective statements in my daily life. Similar to my approach with reframing, I gently held myself accountable for using just one affective statement per day. This could be at home or work. Some simple statements I made noting both positive and negative emotions were "I am annoyed that you left all of the kitchen cabinets open" or "I am frustrated that some of you are not following directions" and "I am excited we did a great job with our math centers today" or "I am proud of your decision and effort to prepare well for your algebra test". Did these statements help me? Absolutely. As the researchers found out, simply naming what I was feeling helped me immensely. If I was naming a negative or challenging emotion, I felt somehow empowered in that expression. The people I was speaking to may have had no idea that their behavior was contributing to a difficult emotion I was experiencing. When I was expressing positive affect, it helped me and others bask in that great feeling a bit longer and with purpose when it was connected to something that someone was doing. I realized I could be helpful in my use of affective statements and show others how to use them as well.

This practice has had positive ripple effects in both my home and work life. Others around me have learned how to use affective language, and it's enormously helpful to empower children to navigate conflicts independently with the use of affective language. These are examples of actual affective statements I have used.

Managing Ourselves Matters ♦ 97

| I feel annoyed that you are not listening to me. | I am excited that we are accomplishing our goals today. | I am frustrated that you are not doing your job. | I am proud of you for treating someone else in a respectful way. |

Figure 4.5 Examples of affective statements.

In my classroom, I use an old wooden toy chest as a "Talk It Out Bench". Posted next to the bench is a sign with sentence stems to help my students use affective language when they are talking about difficult situations and working to resolve everyday conflicts. It helps enormously! With these supports, I have seen my students grow in their ability to express their feelings connected to actions and learn to work through challenging everyday moments. Here is the sign from our classroom.

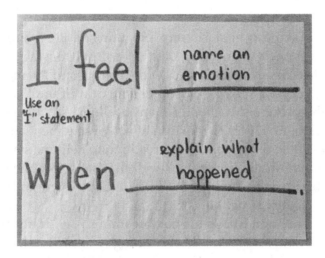

Figure 4.6 Affective language sign in classroom.

How will you harness the power of affective language in your self-management moments? Embracing and practicing an effective strategy will leave you better prepared for challenging situations.

Embrace box breathing. One of the most powerful tools for in-the-moment self-management I have found is box breathing. No wonder. US Navy Seals use box breathing as a technique to stay calm in stressful situations. When we are experiencing stress or extreme sadness or anger, we can use box breathing to help stay calm. I love this simple and easy-to-use technique that can be accessed anytime, anywhere, with our always present and incredibly powerful breath.

Figure 4.7 Box breathing.

When I feel the need to start a box breathing series, I find it helpful to either close my eyes or fix my gaze on a set point. If this happens at home, I can usually close my eyes easily and let the feeling and the moment pass. If I am in my car, I choose a fixed point if possible or wait until I can safely pull over to start the process. In school, if I am dealing with a frustrating situation in my classroom, I'll try to make an affective statement and then let my students know I'll be doing some box breathing to help me stay calm. I have a sign in my room on the upper back wall that says "See the Good. Be the Good". I use this as an anchor when it's needed; it also grounds me in trying to see the best in every situation.

One of the best uses I have for box breathing is with my students during transitions in the classroom. Box breathing is calm; it immediately slows everything down and demands focus of anyone doing it. I added a sensory component to the breathing routine by asking my students to draw a box in the air with their fingers when they breathe. Some students then suggested that they trace a box shape with their fingers on the desk or the carpet where they are working. What great ideas! A bonus was that the large gathering carpet in my classroom was made up of colorful boxes. My students loved using box breathing to get calm, and some even used it in our calming corner on their own. Great times to think about using box breathing are at busy transition times such as before dismissal, after recess, before or after a quiz, or when things just get too loud and energy is too high or after something high-energy or fun has happened. The beauty of box breathing is that once you know how to do it, you'll have it with you forever. It's low-tech and incredibly powerful. Box breathing is a powerful in-the-moment strategy for self-regulation.

A Reflective Strategy for Self-Management

Identify triggers and forgive yourself. The most powerful reflective strategy I use for self-management is, once again, simply the rearview mirror. The images it produces are accurate and clear. When I am brave enough to face them, I can dive deeply into what happened when I failed to manage myself well. From my experience, this work needs to happen well after self-management failures. When I don't manage myself well, I tend to experience disappointment and sadness about it, so I really need to be attuned to when I can move beyond those emotions to engage in this practice.

In *Fostering Resilient Learners*, Kristin Souers and Pete Hall write and share stories about the almost magical, mystical power of grace and how it can transform lives. They write: "Grace can be life altering.... We must teach ourselves to access the attributes necessary to show grace: intentionality, patience, tolerance, understanding, empathy and kindness are a great place to start" (Souers and Hall, pp. 174 and 175). The power of forgiveness and grace and the need to show it to the adults we work with, as well as the students we teach, is almost impossible to describe. The more we practice, the better we get at it; it's as simple as that. The better we get at it, the more delightful our schools and classrooms will be.

Here are several examples of everyday triggers and my reflections about them. I analyzed each situation and worked to deeply understand it so I can avoid making the same mistakes in similar situations again.

Identifying Triggers

WHAT: I yelled at my kids at breakfast before we even left the house. **WHY:** I had a big presentation that day and was feeling insecure about it so I snapped at them for no reason. **FUTURE FIX:** Make a proactive affective statement to your family the night before about it, ask for grace the next day.	**WHAT:** I humiliated a student for a poor behavior choice in front of others. **WHY:** I took it personally. **FUTURE FIX:** Check your mindset, assume best intentions and practice quiet and private feedback to limit shame and preserve student dignity.	**WHAT:** I stopped the science lesson in the middle of it because it was too chaotic. **WHY:** I didn't plan adequately and review expectations with my students. **FUTURE FIX:** Check expectations, realize there will be noise and activity in a hands-on investigation and establish clear expectations.	**WHAT:** I walked into the house and ate 15 cookies in 5 minutes. **WHY:** I didn't eat lunch all day. **FUTURE FIX:** Store healthy snacks at work so you can grab them on the run as you work even if you don't get a chance to stop and eat. Have water and snacks on hand in your car for the way home.

Figure 4.8 Identifying triggers.

Self-management is big, layered, important, nuanced, and at times overwhelming. It's needed on a daily basis. It is the epidermis of our existence as human beings, covering our entire self, visible to others at all times and necessary for our survival. Our skills grow and stretch over time. Self-management impacts ourselves and those around us deeply. Leaning into developing our self-management skills in an organized and intentional way will help us be able to do it better. How will you start today?

Figure 4.9 Building up our SEL skills.

 Reflection Questions

It's time to reflect on and process the information we are learning. Feel free to go back into the chapter to dig into some of these ideas. You can answer these questions by thinking about them, recording ideas in a journal, adding notes here, or creating audio or video notes.

TABLE 4.8 Link and QR code for the online reflection journal

I created an online tool with Google Jamboard that you can also access and use on your own if you'd like to. You can access it below. When you access the file, you'll be asked if you want to make a copy of the file. Say "yes" and this file will be in your Google Drive for you to use and refer back to throughout your reading of the text.		
Resource	**Bitly Link to Access**	**QR Code to Access**
"Embracing Adult SEL" Google Jamboard Reflection Journal	https://bit.ly/EASELjournal1-4	

TABLE 4.9 Reflection activity: Self-management

Explain self-management. Share at least three ideas.		
Idea #1	**Idea #2**	**Idea #3**

TABLE 4.10 Reflection activity: Proactive strategies for self-management

Identify three proactive strategies you can use to develop and maintain your practice of self-management. How will you use each one?		
Strategy #1	**Strategy #2**	**Strategy #3**
What?	What?	What?
How?	How?	How?

TABLE 4.11 Reflection activity: Affective language

Identify a situation where you didn't manage yourself effectively. What happened and what could you have done differently?
What happened?
What could you have done differently?
What affective language could you have used in the situation?

TABLE 4.12 Reflection activity: Box breathing

Describe "box breathing". Then identify a time where box breathing could have been useful. Practice three rounds of box breathing and see how you feel.		
Describe box breathing	**When could you have used it?**	**Practice three rounds. How do you feel?**

5

Moving from Self to Others
Empathy is Curious, Connected, and Active

This is why I teach. Because of moments like this.

One day I was getting ready to work with some students after lunch. The students come into one space from different locations. One student came in crying. I asked if they were OK, they said no. I asked them if they wanted to take a break, have a minute, or get a drink of water. They said no again. I quietly nodded and just watched. Another student said, "Mrs. Turner, they are sad because their brother died and some kids were talking about it at lunch". I said OK, thanks for letting me know. The upset student stayed and got started with the learning activity. When I was moving around to check in on groups and provide support and feedback, the upset student asked me if I wanted to know what happened. I said yes and knelt down next to their desk so I could be at eye level and listen attentively. They let me know that when the death of their brother was brought up at lunch, another student said they didn't care that their sibling had died. This made them incredibly upset. I was so glad they were able to share this with me and told them that I was really sorry they had to go through that and that it must be very hard to lose a brother and that I would also be upset if someone said that to me. They nodded, teary, and kept working. The student next to them then simply said, "_____, I got your back" with the student's name. The upset student nodded and kept working. I was so moved by this small gesture of the supportive student and by the enormous strength and poise of the upset student who kept working. The words of the supportive student were simple yet powerful. I thanked the other student for being supportive and told the student

DOI: 10.4324/9781003458968-6

who lost a sibling that I also had their back. They said thank you Mrs. Turner and kept working. If I had pressed them to tell me what was going on when I initially noticed they were crying, I don't think they would have shared the story with me. When I created space and waited, it allowed the student to share on their terms. This was important to notice.

This moment stopped me cold in my tracks for so many reasons. It was all about empathy. Powerfully and simply, it was about being truly empathetic and feeling with another human being during a time of struggle. I was grateful that my student felt safe enough to share what was upsetting them with me. I work hard to establish authentic relationships with students so that when we encounter tough moments, we can get through them instead of checking out or going around them. I so appreciated the other student who correctly read the moment and provided the simple statement of support. I was in awe of my student who kept working, the best option for them at the moment. If we can create conditions where students will share their pain and their vulnerability and other students recognize and respond to it in a supportive way, with action, then we're going to be OK. We're going to create spaces where kids want to be and where they will learn.

This is also why I teach. Years ago, one of my students came to school wearing the same clothes three days in a row. By the third day, her clothes were extremely wrinkled and dirty, and she looked exhausted, like she might collapse. She had huge bags under her eyes. When she arrived on that third morning, she went to the back of the room to the cubbies where students store their coats, bookbags, and lunches and just stood there, almost wobbly, staring at the cubbies. I think a feather would have knocked her over. She was on the verge of tears, looking almost incapable of functioning. I asked her if she was OK, and she wailed "Noooooo!". So I asked her if she needed to sleep. She nodded. Then she curled up on a small Philadelphia Phillies carpet in the back of the room. The rest of the students arrived for the day and, as needed, stepped over her while she slept. They knew. They knew that this student was not OK and needed to sleep. They didn't ask why, they didn't wake her up, and they didn't complain that they wanted to sleep too. They just knew and when the student woke up later and joined the class, they responded with kindness and open arms. My tired student was able to function. Everyone correctly read the moment and responded in a way that was supportive, not harmful. It was empathy in action. All of us know firsthand how hard it is to function when we are tired. We understood.

Later that week, the student shared with me that lots of relatives live in her home, and she doesn't always get a good place to sleep, so sometimes she has to sleep on the floor or on the couch and can't get a good night's sleep. That's why she arrived in a state that wasn't learning-ready. I knew I'd never get to her to learn if I didn't attend to her most basic needs first. The beauty of the responses of the other students reminded me that when we work hard to understand what others might be going through and model for children how to respond, they understand as well, and they know how to do it when needed. Kids understand empathy and want to show it.

What Is Social Awareness?

Let's head back to the dictionary to construct some meaning of this phrase.

TABLE 5.1 Definitions of social and awareness

Social	*Marked by or passed in pleasant* **companionship** *with* **friends** *or* **associates**
Awareness	**Knowledge and understanding** *that something is happening or exists*

From these meanings, we can put together a definition of social awareness that might sound something like "knowledge and understanding of friends and associates".

To me, social awareness is all about movement: moving out toward others, moving to make our view wider. It's growing outward from a focus on just ourselves to a focus with a wider lens that includes others, understanding what is happening and knowing how someone might feel or what they need. It's also about knowledge and understanding of bigger issues, such as social issues. When we understand the circumstances and feelings of others, we can harness our superpower to be supportive in simple and extraordinary ways. At times, it means suspending the act of feeding our own needs and giving to others. At times, this is born from a connection, the power of having gone through something that someone else is facing and knowing firsthand, personally and viscerally, what they feel. In a complex world, it's critical that we grow our empathy muscles and live in empathy so we can bridge the divides that separate us and move forward. It's necessary for us to be socially aware if we are going to grow our social emotional learning (SEL) skills and model them for others. Our Adult SEL journey continues with social awareness.

Casel defines social awareness as

> "the abilities to understand the perspectives of and empathize with others, including those from diverse backgrounds, cultures, and contexts. This includes the capacities to feel compassion for others, understand broader historical and social norms for behavior in different settings, and recognize family, school, and community resources and support."

Social awareness helps us understand and use empathy and become aware of social norms and customs across cultures. With social awareness, we learn to express compassion for others and demonstrate that actively. This helps us see and appreciate individuals as human beings with a set of feelings and beliefs instead of merely someone who is different from us. With empathy muscles and broader perspective, we develop ways to be supportive both at home and in the workplace. This is critically important in schools, where diverse groups of adults and students gather to live, work, and learn together. It is exciting to explore strategies to strengthen social awareness. With this work, we are in the Confidence Zone of SEL, understanding how to engage in strategies that support our skill development and help us live in SEL.

Proactive Strategies for Social Awareness

What are some proactive strategies to support social awareness both personally and professionally? Here are some of my favorites. They have been incredibly powerful for me as I have worked to grow my skills over the years.

Understand and Embrace Empathy. What Does Empathy Mean?

TABLE 5.2 Definition of empathy

Empathy	The action of understanding, being **aware of, being sensitive to, and vicariously experiencing the feelings, thoughts, and experience of another** .... *without having the feelings, thoughts, and experience fully communicated in an objectively explicit manner*

Empathy involves inferring. From a young age, we learn the classic analogy that empathy is all about walking in someone else's shoes. This is a great metaphor for people of all ages. Thinking about what it feels like when you are experiencing a challenge or difficult emotion is something that spurs deep thinking in us about others. It may move us to action. When we see someone feeling sad, disappointed, or upset, we can say to ourselves: "I know what that feels like, it is really hard". What we do next, though, is where we meet a fork in the road and sympathy and empathy take a different path.

The dictionary also says

> "*Sympathy* and *empathy* both refer to a caring response to the emotional state of another person, but a distinction between them is typically

made: while *sympathy* is a feeling of sincere concern for someone who is experiencing something difficult or painful, *empathy* involves actively sharing in the emotional experience of the other person."

To truly understand and be empathetic, we have to understand that empathy is different from sympathy. Both involve perspective and understanding what someone is experiencing. But the sympathetic response is passive. With it, we may say to ourselves things like "I feel so bad about this", "I am sorry for that person", or "Gee, that really sucks". With an empathetic response, we are active. I believe true empathy is active. We feel what another person is going through, we start to have some of that same pain or joy that another is experiencing, and we act on it.

Empathy is active. Once we understand what someone else is experiencing, especially if it is difficult, empathy won't do much good unless we act on it. I know you have lots of examples of this in your personal and professional life. The examples I shared earlier from my classroom both involved action. People in both situations acted to show support with a goal of making the situation better for the one hurting. I believe that in order to really live and walk in empathy, we need to act. We can model this in our personal and professional lives in lots of ways. Empathy is active.

When one of our teenage kids comes home in a terrible mood from school, work, a sporting event, or social situation, I can read that mood and understand that things are not going well and ask my kids if they need anything. I can tell them I love them and offer to make a grilled cheese sandwich, one of the few things I can cook. I can give them space if needed. Before I really understood empathy, I may have panicked and been afraid of messing up, so I would hide from their moods or even make things worse by saying the wrong things. Saying a few things that are supportive or even slipping a note of support that simply says "I love you" under a closed door can do wonders.

A few years ago, one of my students would always arrive in class on Monday mornings in tough shape. They were late. They were sluggish, moving slowly, and often teary, and this would make engaging in learning really, really difficult on Monday mornings. Because they were late, they would often miss our joyful, inclusive morning ritual, our morning roundup. When they arrived, they would sit and do nothing. I knew I needed to figure out how to help my student be more successful on Mondays. I had to do some investigating, however. I needed to bring an authentic curiosity to the situation to build understanding and a plan to move forward. So I started with asking questions.

Empathy is curious. Because Mondays were hard for this student, I did some work on other days of the week. I had a check-in conversation on a

Tuesday or Wednesday when they were regulated and asked why Mondays were so difficult. This student was usually more regulated on those days as we got into our week, so this was a better time to try to figure out what was going on. They told me that their parents were separated, and Sunday night was their night with their parent that they did not see much. Because they didn't see each other all week, they stayed up late, hanging out, watching movies, and playing video games. Then their Monday morning ritual was to go to a fast-food restaurant drive-through for breakfast together. They said a lot of times the line was long and it made them late for school but they still loved it because they were with their parent that they rarely saw.

As I reflected on what I was learning, I stayed out of judgment. Empathy is curious. I could immediately relate to how difficult his situation was as I am a child of divorced parents. I knew firsthand the pain of moving back and forth between homes. In my childhood, when my parents separated, they first agreed to each leave our family home and stay in a nearby apartment for a month at a time so my siblings and I could stay in one place. But one of our parents quickly broke that agreement and would not leave our house. While my other parent needed time to pull together the resources to live on their own, we all lived together in a situation that was toxic. Then, when they did finally split up, our house was sold and each parent moved into a smaller home. Every three months, the kids switched houses, and while we were at one parent's home, every other weekend we had to go and live with the other parent. If it sounds crazy, that's because it was! We would routinely leave homework, sneakers, keys, bikes, and lots of other things at the wrong house. We spent time walking and biking between the houses. This was emotionally exhausting and stressful. No doubt, it impacted how we all showed up at school.

When my student shared his situation with me, I immediately said: "I am so sorry you are going through this. I know how hard it is when your parents split up and you have to spend time in two places. My parents were divorced when I was a kid, and it was really, really hard to go back and forth. I am so grateful you have shared this with me". My questions to my student about what was hard on Monday morning were curious. My vulnerability in sharing was active. When we are curious and active, we grow our capacity to truly embrace and express empathy. Curiosity increases our knowledge, and action provides practice to increase our skills. Both curiosity and action breed connection.

Mapping to curiosity and action. The Casel definition of social awareness includes the following concepts as well. It helped me to map each of them to the ideas of being curious and active so I can live in empathy in as many concrete ways as possible. It provides me with a specific roadmap for practicing empathy. Concepts mapped to curiosity demand robust questions. Concepts mapped to action foster awareness and authentic practice.

TABLE 5.3 Empathy mapping

Concept	Mapping	Thinking deeply
Taking others' perspectives	Curiosity	What is someone else thinking or going through? I need to ask questions.
Recognizing strengths in others	Action	Identifying strengths with a proactive, strength-based practice
Demonstrating empathy and compassion	Active	Doing and saying things that help; supportive practice when needed
Understanding and expressing gratitude	Action	Research-based positive practice that can be routinized
Identifying diverse social norms, including unjust ones	Curiosity	Learning what I can about culture and identity, understanding social issues and "othering"
Showing concern for the feelings of others	Action	Connecting practice: checking in, validating, supporting
Recognizing situational demands and opportunities	Curiosity and action	What is going on? What can I do? How can I help, support? What knowledge and/or skills do I need?
Understanding the influences of organizations and systems on behavior	Curiosity	What are norms in various settings? How do they differ? What does this mean for individuals and groups? What data can I review that reveals patterns and trends?

Practice empathy. When we deeply understand empathy, we can make proactive, specific plans to practice it. This involves identifying the specific moves we need to make both personally and professionally and holding ourselves accountable for living them.

Last year, my husband and I were talking about how socializing after Covid has been just, well, different. It's harder. We both acknowledged that we want to be more social but that somehow it feels more challenging after Covid. As a seasoned adult, I still feel, at times, nervous when entering social situations, even when I know most people there. I wonder if anyone will talk to me, find me interesting, or think well of me. I think these are all normal, human reactions, but I wanted to figure out how to get through them. My husband shared his strategy for any work or personal social situation.

He said these two words so calmly, so simply, I almost had to laugh. He said, "Ask questions".

Ask questions. When we are in a situation where we are not sure what to do and we want to avoid silence, we can ask questions. Here are some basic but powerful, connecting questions. Empathy is connected. Like so many, I avoid discussion of religion and politics in casual social settings. Even with this restriction, there is so much to talk about!

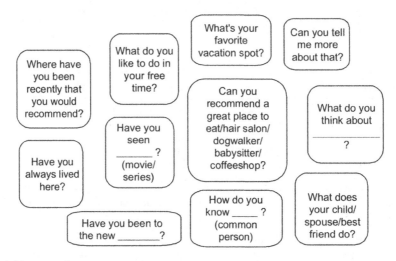

Figure 5.1 Asking questions.

We can also ask questions in the classroom. Gathering rituals for students and adults of all ages go so far in creating connections. Whether I am running a morning meeting with elementary students, facilitating a round-up in secondary school, or facilitating a day of professional learning for educators, I always use a connection question to help us authentically come together.

Create curiosity conversations. Recently, I was running a full-day workshop with educators; over 50 people were present. The sheer numbers might turn one off to the idea of connecting intentionally with a circle. I embraced the moment. We circled up to start our day and used a talking piece, much like we would in a classroom. I was actively modeling the classroom practice I wanted them to learn about. Passing around the talking piece, I asked everyone to share one thing they were good at. We quickly all realized we were in a room full of experts! People shared strengths in education, hobbies, positivity practices, grandparenting, organization skills, physical feats, and more. I was in awe. I knew we needed the connection to root us in togetherness as we spent a day learning about trauma, SEL, and how we could work to grow our practice of supporting our learners. It was a beautiful opening connection.

Another early part of the day had us sharing "A Rose and Thorn". Participants were asked to share one thing going well and one thing that was difficult, personally or professionally. They wrote these on an index card and then we shared by walking silently around the room, showing each other our vulnerable truths on those cards, and learning about others in the process while calm music played. Thank you Kristin Souers for sharing this powerful practice with me! After we did this, we played a simple game of "4 Corners". I asked participants to go to a corner in the room labeled with a feeling. The choices were connected, affirmed, surprised, or anxious.

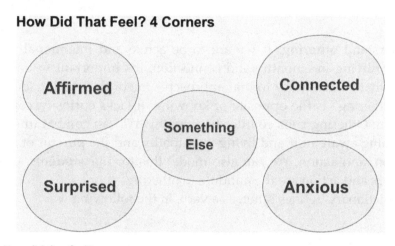

Figure 5.2 How did that feel?

The largest numbers of participants went to the connected and affirmed corners. Wow! I was blown away by this simple activity. By sharing, they connected with each other. As we made our way through the workshop together, our connection helped us learn and grow in a more powerful way. I reminded everyone how powerful this would be in a classroom. When people of all ages can articulate what's good and also hard in their lives, we normalize all of it. We accept all of it. From there, we can grow in empathy by activating our curiosity and putting our knowledge into action with support. This is also a simple and effective way to learn about others.

One of the most powerful curiosity conversations I was ever part of involved a faculty meeting. What? A faculty meeting? Yes! A faculty meeting I attended years ago was one of the most powerful empathy moments I have ever experienced as an adult. This extraordinary faculty meeting at my elementary school was a game changer. It taught me that the SEL we do with our students is just as important for adults. In a nutshell, our administrators created the space and conditions for vulnerable sharing by reading the children's book *If She Only Knew Me* and then asking us a question. You can read about this powerful experience in a blog I wrote for Ed Post in 2018.

TABLE 5.4 Link and QR code "How Opening Up to My Colleagues…."

Resource	Link to Access	QR Code to Access
Blog: "How Opening Up to My Colleagues Made Me Realize Social Emotional Learning Isn't Just For Students"	https://bit.ly/EASELfaculty	

Understand othering. If we are to be active and intentional with our practice of living in empathy and connection, it's important to understand concepts that run contrary to that approach. One of them is the idea of othering. "Othering" is the opposite of knowing. It lacks curiosity, connection, and action. Othering runs counter to empathy. We can combat this practice by becoming aware of it and living in empathy and the pursuit of curiosity, connection, and action. We can also model this for our students. Curiosity, connection, and action are the antidote to othering.

The dictionary defines other, as a verb, in the following way.

TABLE 5.5 Definition of othering

Other	**To** *treat or* **consider** *(a person or a group of people) as* **alien to oneself** *or one's group (as because of different racial, sexual, or cultural characteristics)*

When we classify ourselves and others into identities and don't work to see the commonalities we share, we other. When we perceive ourselves as better than a group, we other. When we label, we other.

Kendra Cherry writes in "How Othering Contributes to Discrimination and Prejudice",

> "Othering is a phenomenon in which some individuals or groups are defined and labeled as not fitting in within the norms of a social group. It is an effect that influences how people perceive and treat those who are viewed as being part of the in-group versus those who are seen as being part of the out-group."

Othering can include labeling according to age, skin color, religion, sexual orientation, gender identity, socioeconomic status, and political affiliation. She then writes,

"In many cases, people 'other' those that they do not actually know. Lack of personal knowledge and contact with people can lead to assumptions about them. This makes it easier to perceive them as overwhelmingly different or even less human."

This is an excellent resource to help you understand the concept of othering. I highly recommend reading it in its entirety to learn more.

TABLE 5.6 QR code and Link to "What is Othering?"

Resource	Link to Access	QR Code to Access
Article: "How Othering Contributes to Discrimination and Prejudice"	https://bit.ly/EASELothering	

By becoming aware of the existence of the practice of othering, we can combat it. Often rooted in personal bias, which many people are not aware of, othering pulls people apart instead of connecting them together. Gaining knowledge, asking questions, including people, and seeing our commonalities can help us avoid this damaging phenomenon.

In-the-Moment Strategy for Social Awareness

Respond with empathy. I was brought to my knees as a parent during Covid-19. One day our kids, ages 13 and 14, were going to school, and the next they were not. One was attending zoom classes every day, which lulled them into an anxious, zombie-like mess. Another child was doing asynchronous work while sitting in bed clutching a teddy bear one minute and doing something close to punching a wall the next. It was not good. It was not fun. Like so many others, I felt like I was losing my mind while I tried to stay connected to our kids. And on top of all of it, I was a teacher.

During this time, we relied on family walks for exercise and routine. We saw other families on our walks, and while none of us really looked happy, we were doing it because we knew it was connected to mental health and got us moving in the warm spring weather. We did this even though our kids relentlessly showed us TikTok videos of teens complaining about this new phenomenon, the family walk. While I hoped we'd find connection and laughter, we were mostly silent, going through the motions. But we did it anyway, with our sweet German shepherd Bella, and I am sure it helped us each in some small different way.

Around this time, one of our kids was really struggling socially. They were not successful in keeping relationships, and like so many teenagers, they were being dropped by their social group. On top of regular teen emotions and hormones and the pandemic, this produced difficult and devastating emotions that lasted a very long time. Quite frankly, I didn't know how to respond; in fact, I believe many of my early attempts at connection and listening actually made things worse.

After months of struggling with how to respond, I did what I often do when I need help: I looked for something to read. Fortunately for me, I found an incredibly powerful resource that spoke to me in a simple way and helped me to change my behavior. I read the beautiful and brilliant article "7 Ways to Respond to Students with Empathy" by Amanda Morin on the Understood website. This article has quite simply changed my life. I am incredibly grateful for Ms. Morin's words and her approach.

Before empathy. Before I read the article, a conversation or walk with my child where I am not responding with empathy might look and sound something like this.

TABLE 5.7 Before empathy

Me	My child
I ask "How are you doing?"	No answer, scowl or response of bad or terrible
I say "Oh no. What's going on?"	Complains of friends who don't return text messages or won't commit to plans or of being removed from a friend's private story on Instagram or seeing "friends" gathering together on the Snapchat snapmap
I ask "Do you really think these people are your friends? Do you think friends should treat you like that?"	Our child responds with something like "Of course, they are my friends! Don't you think I know who my friends are? I hung out with them before. Duh. I can't believe you don't know who my friends are and think I don't know who my friends are."
I say something like "Well at least you have your other friends, you know the ones from work/middle school/camp/etc."	Responds with something like "That doesn't matter. They aren't who I am hanging around with. That doesn't help me out here. I can't believe you are saying this. That's so stupid".
I am now silent and miserable, not helping my child, and I feel terrible and like a failure.	Silent and miserable, not helped

Ms. Morin's simple article outlines seven very specific ways we can respond to students with empathy. Necessary in schools, this approach works well with any human we interact with. Here is what I learned from her.

Understand what the other person needs. Many of us grew up with the reminder to treat others as we would like to be treated. This can turn into an inner voice when we need it to. This is a kind approach as we can generally agree that we all want to be treated well. Except what if what you want or need is not what someone else needs at a particular moment in time? We need to think about what they need. And if we aren't sure what that is, we need to ask. If asking in the moment doesn't work, we want to make sure we ask when the other person is regulated so we can make sure we have that critical information stored for when we need to use it. We need to make the situation about the other person instead of us.

A simple example is thinking about what someone needs when they are upset. Some people need a hug, an arm around a shoulder, or a conversation. Others need to be left alone to work through their feelings. Over the years, I have learned that students need very different things when they are struggling. To know what they need, we need to ask and we need to know how to ask. With key family members and our students, asking in advance and knowing are significant parts of being successful in these moments. In the situation above, I could have asked my child what they needed. If they were quiet or said nothing, I could have just been there in silence with them, without continuing to pry, needle, or put myself needing information first. Finding out what someone needs is rooted in curiosity, a key component of empathy.

Questions matter. We all know what it feels like when we ask basic, yes-or-no questions and we get basic answers. We can feel frustrated! We wonder why our conversation partner is not sharing more, particularly our own children or our students. However, the person we are talking to is doing their job, answering our questions. So to learn what is going on, we have to ask better questions. This practice is rooted in curiosity and is related to connection and action. By working hard to learn how someone is doing, how they are feeling, and avoiding assumptions, we'll be able to authentically empathize and move to supportive action. If we don't ask, we won't know. If we don't ask well, we'll be stuck with basic information and won't be able to act in a powerful way. Asking open-ended questions moves us to a place where we can better support our friend, family member, student, or another person.

Listen first, react later. It is hard not to react. Throughout a day, there are so many situations that we could react to. But if we are truly working to live in empathy, to build trust, and to be supportive, we may need to set aside our reactions. This is rooted in the SEL idea of self-management. So many SEL skills are interconnected. We have to be aware of our thoughts, feelings, and actions first and then we need to manage them. When we are listening to and learning about others, this is critical. Setting aside our own reaction and keeping focus on the person we are supporting can actually preserve the energy we need to do this well. It can actually positively impact our Box of Energy! It ensures that we are making the situation about the other person and not ourselves. This can be so challenging at times. The practice of reflection afterwards can support us in exploring our reactions after the fact. In fact, I highly recommend that when we experience challenging situations, we commit to taking the time to review our reactions and feelings around what happened so we don't become resentful or suppress our feelings in a way that is not healthy. Putting aside our own reactions so we can focus on others is active and a way to live in empathy.

Start with "I". "I statements" help us focus on how we are feeling instead of making other people feel defensive by saying something that starts with "you". This relates to the use of affective statements described earlier; affective statements combine an "I statement" with a feeling and connect it to something that took place. This subtle shift is one that can change a situation from being filled with blame to being one that is filled with support and opens up two-way communication. When we share how someone's choices or reactions make us feel, we are opening up the empathy connection between us. The person we are working to support may have never even thought about how you might feel or how they could have made others feel. When we share our feelings we open up our own humanity and create the conditions for connection. Using "I statements" is both connecting and active.

Listen, listen, listen. Actively listening really, really well is very hard in a distracted world. I'll explore this idea in more detail in Chapter 6 ("Relationship Skills Matter"). But here, we need to understand that we need to really listen. For me, this means stopping, being still, making sure I'm not looking at my phone or watch, nodding along, and really thinking about the information I am hearing without a rush to add a comment and make a connection with a story about me. It means straight-up affirmation. For me, this looks like nodding along with what is being said, keeping my brain quiet, and almost replaying what I am hearing in my head so I can make sure I am truly focused on the person I need to support. This is active and a key part of living in empathy.

Stop fixing things! In a world where I live to complete things, this is a big challenge. As a mom and wife, I run the house, making plans and appointments, washing laundry, pulling weeds, and making sure we have enough toilet paper. As a teacher, I make hundreds of decisions quickly every day in the interest of connecting with my students, completing lessons, assessing skills, covering curriculum, and navigating conflicts. If I stop doing and fixing in either of these roles, I stop making progress. Learning to listen to our children during the pandemic in this way without offering a solution was really, really hard. But it helped and when I stopped doing it and started just being there, things got better. Uncomfortable walks became pleasant bike rides together. I took cues from our kids and didn't really start a conversation, waiting until they chose to tell me something or share what was going on in their lives. Again, this was hard and while it seems to be passive, it was a very intentional and active way to show empathy and be there in support for them. I do the same thing when a student is struggling In my classroom. I ask them if they are OK and what they need to fix something, or instead of demanding action such as an apology, I ask how they can fix something. Things go much better with this approach.

Got feelings? I saw a social media post about feelings that has never left me. It said something like "Feelings are like visitors, they come in, occupy some space, but eventually leave". In working to understand people, I have practiced the skill of asking how someone is feeling or saying "it sounds like you are feeling _____" and then just listening. Sometimes I say something like "That makes so much sense" or "I felt exactly the same way recently", and sometimes I just nod in silence, letting the feelings fill the air before they leave. Validating feelings without judgment is active after curiosity has opened up the feelings themselves. This is another important part of living in empathy.

You can read Ms. Morin's entire article here. I go back to it time and time again and share it in professional development sessions I facilitate. It's a gem.

TABLE 5.8 Link and code for "7 Ways to Respond to Students with Empathy".

Resource	Link to Access	QR Code to Access
Article: "7 Ways to Respond to Students with Empathy"	https://u.org/3OoXWl5	

After empathy. After I read, digested, and internalized the ideas from Ms. Morin's article, a conversation or walk with my child where I am responding with empathy might look and sound more like this.

TABLE 5.8A After empathy

Me	My child
I ask "How are you doing?"	No answer, scowl or response of bad or terrible
I say nothing or "I'm so sorry."	We walk or sit together quietly for a while.
I say "I am sorry things are so tough right now. I remember that high school was so up and down, and when things were down, it was really hard."	Looks at me and nods
I wait a while and then say "If there is anything you need from me or if there is anything I can do, please let me know. I want to help, but I know I can't fix things or make the problems go away. I also don't want to annoy you."	Responds with "OK, thanks." We continue to sit or walk quietly.
After a while, I say "Do you want: • to go out for a coffee? or • a grilled cheese? or • to watch something on Netflix? or • to play fetch with Bella?	Responds with "I'd like to ..." or something like "I think I'm just gonna chill in my room but thanks Mom. I'll be OK."
I say "OK, can I give you a hug?"	Responds with "Yes". We hug.
I simply say "Love you."	Responds with "Love you too."

After this exchange, there is calm and peace between us. We both know the problems won't go away and are not fixed; they may even get worse. But we had a positive, supportive exchange that was steeped in empathy and that was curious, connected, and active. I feel relief inside.

Reflective Strategy for Social Awareness

Think back. To truly reflect on whether or not we used empathy, I think it's important to identify situations where we used empathy and those where we did not and then think about what was similar and different in each. Think specifically about a time when you didn't show empathy at home, work, or school. Here are key questions to ask in this process:

> ★ What did you do?
> ★ What did you say?
> ★ How did you feel?
> ★ How did you make another feel?
> ★ What could you have done differently?

I'll use an example of a situation where I clearly did not use empathy and was incredibly disappointed with myself. Luckily, I paid great attention to how I felt afterward, and it opened up some helpful reflection and the realization that I had not used empathy when I needed to.

This situation was one where, on a Friday morning, a problem presented itself at my elementary school, and I had a great chance to be a flexible, helpful person ... and I blew it. Plain and simple. I was not the best version of myself and didn't show up when I was needed to help out with a challenging situation. At home later that night, I shared the incident with my husband. He had also had a tough day at work, so while we chatted, we reminded each other of the need to pause and consider others' perspectives. Upon reflection, I isolated one key detail of the situation. I had failed to be empathetic. I did not show empathy to the administrator who was trying to solve the operational problem of the lack of a substitute teacher for one who was out. You can read a reflective blog I wrote about this here.

TABLE 5.9 Link and QR code for "December Can Be Tough...."

Resource	Link to Access	QR Code to Access
Blog: "December Can Be Tough. Let's bring Empathy and Grace Into Our Schools in the New Year"	https://bit.ly/EASELdec	

In the situation, I had remained focused on myself and did not consider the needs or positions of others. Empathy matters as much for adults in education as it does for our students. We get better at showing and embodying empathy the more we practice it, just like kids do. This incident reminded me in a powerful way that adults need and require SEL just as much as students do to make our schools succeed. I answered my reflective questions about this situation to help me work through it.

What did you do? When asked to cover an additional class on a Friday morning of December, effectively doubling the number of students I would teach all day, I said no.

What did you say? I told my admin team that I would not assist with class coverage and that it was not my problem or responsibility.

How did you feel? When asked, I felt angry and agitated; then later, I felt shame and embarrassment after I refused to help and others stepped up to assist in the situation.

How did you make another feel? I am not sure, but I wasn't empathetic to my admin team's plight of having to cover classes. I most likely caused others to feel frustrated with my lack of assistance and then worried that they wouldn't be able to fill the need.

What could you have done differently? When initially frustrated, I could have slowed down the situation before I responded. Then I could have responded calmly and said I would assist for the day. While this would have remained a challenge, I could have then talked to my grade-level team to seek assistance and generate some ideas around how I would plan the day with double the number of students I normally teach. As a team, we may have been able to come up with some creative approaches to covering the class, such as sharing responsibility, rotating coverage, or using different, larger areas of the school if they were available. Together, we could have created a better situation.

As you can now see, social awareness is a complex idea and requires us to let go of ourselves. There are many elements that relate to both self-awareness and self-management. We can get better at being socially aware through practice and intentional focus. I am not perfect, but rather, better, at being socially aware and supporting others around me. This brings me happiness and satisfaction, which help keep my Box of Energy big and full for other needs. When I empathize and support others well, I am also practicing elements of my own self-awareness, and the positive vibes that come with it reduce the need to manage myself. With practice, you'll grow your skills as well, and these strategies will become second nature and be part of who you are and how you live.

Moving from Self to Others ◆ 121

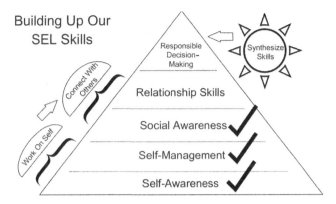

Figure 5.3 Building up our SEL skills.

 Reflection Questions

It's time to reflect on and process the information we are learning. Feel free to go back into the chapter to dig into some of these ideas. You can answer these questions by thinking about them, recording ideas in a journal, adding notes here, or creating audio or video notes.

TABLE 5.10 Link and QR code for the online reflection journal

I created an online tool with Google Jamboard that you can also access and use on your own if you'd like to. You can access it below. When you access the file, you'll be asked if you want to make a copy of the file. Say "yes" and this file will be in your Google Drive for you to use and refer back to throughout your reading of the text.		
Resource	**Link to Access**	**QR Code to Access**
"Embracing Adult SEL" Google Jamboard Reflection Journal	https://bit.ly/EASELjournal5-8	

TABLE 5.11 Reflection activity: Social awareness

Explain social awareness. Use at least three ideas.		
Idea #1	**Idea #2**	**Idea #3**

TABLE 5.12 Reflection activity: fostering social awareness

Identify three proactive strategies you can try to foster positive social awareness. Which three are they? Why are you choosing them?		
Strategy #1	**Strategy #2**	**Strategy #3**
What?	What?	What?
Why?	Why?	Why?

TABLE 5.13 Reflection activity: Lacking empathy

Describe a recent personal situation where you didn't use empathy. What could you have done differently to show empathy and achieve a different, and most likely better, outcome. What did you do?
Describe the situation.
What did you do?
What did you say?
How did you feel?
How did you make another feel?
What could you have done differently?

TABLE 5.14 Reflection activity: Empathy is curious, connected, and active

Empathy is curious, connected, and active. Share an idea around each of these elements you'll focus on to grow your social awareness going forward.		
Curious	**Connected**	**Active**

6

Relationship Skills Matter
Grow Connections with Everyday Practices

In 2021, school started virtually. I was teaching second grade online and working to establish strong connections with my students and their families and also needed to help my students connect and form relationships with each other. This was hard but with the power of innovation it was possible. We had virtual morning meetings, breakout room chats, and fun activities like scavenger hunts and pet guests on zoom while we were doing school.

To connect with families early in the year, I created a survey for adults to fill out that asked how Covid had impacted their family, what the strengths of their child were, what holidays each family celebrated, what language was their first, and more. Families shared that they celebrated various holidays which were wonderful to see. I loved the diversity in our classroom community. I believe this simple survey helped me establish strong connections with families in spite of the challenging situation we all faced with online learning. Throughout the year, I held weekly family zoom meetings to provide updates about school, answer questions, and build community. I provided a weekly newsletter that shared what we were learning. All of this helped me to create solid relationships with my students' families.

For the past several years, I had been working to be more culturally responsive by ensuring that any celebrations we had in class were inclusive of various cultures and avoided naming celebrations for specific holidays such as Halloween, Christmas, and Easter. I make sure I taught my students about various holidays and cultural celebrations. I use Nearpod, an online learning tool, and Readworks, a digital literacy tool, to help with this goal. Both have fantastic, inclusive resources that are tailored for all ages K–12. Here's a list of some of the celebrations and holidays we learned about. In our learning, I worked to make sure our learning includes these elements when possible: holiday origins, type of celebration, and traditions.

TABLE 6.1 Holidays and celebrations

Fall Celebrations	Winter Holidays	Spring Celebrations
Rosh Hashanah	Hanukkah	Ramadan
Halloween	Kwanzaa	Eid-al-Fitr
Día de los Muertos	Christmas	Passover
Diwali	Winter Solstice & New Year	Easter
Thanksgiving	Chinese New Year	First day of spring

During the fall, as many young people do, lots of students shared with excitement their plans to dress up for Halloween, what costumes they were going to wear, and their plans for trick-or-treating. One student did not share this and I realized this family did not celebrate Halloween. I consulted the family survey from earlier in the year to confirm this and realized this was the case. Armed with this information, I wanted to be sensitive to the situation of Halloween being discussed at school. While Halloween is a topic of conversation for many, I did not want this student to feel excluded or othered in the midst of this. I intentionally avoided Halloween-themed activities, instead focusing on Fall. I let my students know that not everyone celebrated Halloween. Many were surprised to hear this.

Spring arrived and I was very depleted. I was exhausted and not at my best after starting school virtually, continuing to work through the pandemic, and then having to teach with a hybrid flexible (or HyFlex) model better known as "room and zoom". This way of teaching was incredibly draining and difficult to do well. I had students that remained at home and two cohorts of students who each came in 2 days a week. It was beyond challenging. I knew this and as we lurched toward Spring Break, I ran out of time to teach about all of the holidays I had intended to. I was able to get in my lesson about Passover and Easter but not the lesson on Ramadan. I knew this was an oversight on my part. I felt terrible about this but had to just keep moving forward and planned to teach it when we returned from Spring Break.

Shortly after that, Eid, the end of the holy month of Ramadan, arrived on the calendar. I received an email from a frustrated parent who communicated that their child patiently listened and learned about Christmas, Passover, Kwanzaa, and Diwali but never enjoyed a classroom lesson on Ramadan or Eid-al-Fitr or had a teacher wish them "Eid Mubarak", the traditional greeting to celebrate the "feast of fast-breaking" at the end of the Ramadan holy month. I was stopped cold in my tracks. I felt horrible. I had let my student and family down because I hadn't truly lived in social awareness around this element of culture. My practice was less sharp than it should have been. My skills were not as developed as they needed to be.

To work to repair my error, that day I got a card and wrote a message to wish my student "Eid Mubarak", meaning blessed festival. I dropped it off at their home and wrote back to apologize profusely to the family. My student loved the card, and I received a message from their parent that it was deeply appreciated. On the Monday, when we returned from Spring Break, I did the lesson on Ramadan with my students to welcome them back, explaining that I had failed to teach the lesson because I ran out of time. I communicated an apology to all of my students. As I do with other holidays, I asked students to share family traditions and how they celebrated Ramadan and Eid. This student shined with pride as they shared their family traditions. I'll never forget this moment in time and vowed to make sure I teach many cultural holiday lessons each year to affirm diverse identity and culture in my classroom.

This is where social awareness and relationship skills intersected in my social emotional learning (SEL) world. Although this was an uncomfortable moment for me, a failure of sorts, my strong relationship with the family helped me navigate this moment and work through my shortcomings. I realized as well that I lacked social awareness around celebrating this important holiday in the Muslim calendar. Without the authentic relationship and regular communication I engaged in with my families, this situation may have ended differently with a higher degree of frustration and anger that could have lingered and smoldered the rest of the school year. It could have negatively impacted my students' learning. This taught me it's absolutely critical to be culturally responsive for our students.

We live in a matrix. Yes we do. You heard me right. We live in a matrix of relationships that is constantly growing, changing, shape-shifting, and challenging us to act based on various forces and influences. Success in this matrix demands knowledge and skills. This is especially true in education as we work to make positive connections and navigate relationships with students, their families and caregivers, our co-workers, administrators, school support staff, and the greater community. We have so many relationships to attend to. It can be overwhelming to think about at times. However, as with the other SEL competencies we have learned about, we can identify specific skills and moves that can help us to be more successful in our relationships both personally and professionally.

What are Relationship Skills?

Once again, let's visit the dictionary to help us make sense of the phrase "relationship skills".

TABLE 6.2 Definitions of relationship and skill

Relationship	The **relation connecting** or binding **participants** *in a relationship: such as kinship*
Skill	A **learned power** *of doing something* **competently**: *a developed aptitude or* **ability**

From these meanings, we can put together a definition that might sound something like this: relationship skills are the "ability to have connecting relations with others".

Casel defines relationship skills as

"the abilities to establish and maintain healthy and supportive relationships and to effectively navigate settings with diverse individuals and groups. This includes the capacities to communicate clearly, listen actively, cooperate, work collaboratively to problem solve, and negotiate conflict constructively, navigate settings with differing social and cultural demands and opportunities, provide leadership, and seek or offer help when needed."

Additional concepts related to relationship skills include communicating effectively, positive relationships, demonstrating cultural competency, practicing teamwork and collaborative problem-solving, resolving conflicts constructively, resisting negative social pressure, showing leadership in groups, seeking or offering support and help when needed, and standing up for the rights of others.

By now, we know that the SEL competencies we are learning about and practicing are intertwined. The Casel framework lays out five competencies as well as the various settings and stakeholders who engage in work on them. There are lots of overlapping ideas and connections among the competencies. Generally, I believe that when we have strong self-awareness and self-management and we are socially aware, we enjoy authentic, positive, and strong relationships.

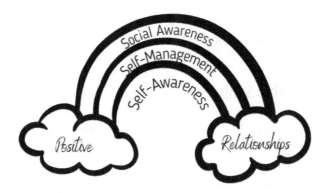

Figure 6.1 Positive relationships.

In my experience, I have found that people generally enjoy being around others who are aware of and can manage themselves and their thoughts and feelings. I know firsthand how hard it is to be around people who lack these skills. The care and understanding that one possesses when they have social awareness feed relationships in a positive way. Self-awareness is at the heart of it all; without this quality, it's very difficult to move into effective self-management and embrace social awareness. Without deep knowledge of ourselves (as we explored in Chapters 1 and 2), it would be difficult to become authentically socially aware. These competencies directly feed into relationship skills.

As I work to successfully navigate myriad relationships in my life, I have come to realize we are always growing in our relationships. We have connections that come and go, those that seem to occupy a moment in time and those that are eternal. As educators, we have some that last just a school year and others that are more enduring. It all makes sense. I like to think about the word "grow" deeply as I continue to nurture and make sense of my relationships. Each letter can stand for a powerful idea in the complicated and exciting world of relationships.

We Continually GROW in our Relationships

We are always......

- G - Gathering Relationships
- R - Retaining Relationships
- O - Offboarding Relationships
- W - Wondering about Relationships

Figure 6.2 Growing in relationships.

Gathering. Throughout our lives, we gather relationships as we live and move through our experiences and the world. A relationship can be small but powerful like one with the employee at your local coffee shop, the facilities employee who cleans and maintains the space you work in, or the neighbor who smiles and waves when you pass by. These relationships can be new and exciting. A friend met at a school event, your place of worship, or the community center or gym or on the sidelines of your child's sports event or in the audience of the school play can create deep, shared connections. They can help us when we least expect it, teach us, and enable us to learn and grow, leaving us changed for the better in their wake. The key to finding them is being open and aware when opportunities to connect arise.

In this day and age, I find myself constantly telling our children to "Look up". I also need to remind myself to do this. Because we are all pretty much addicted to our phones and technology, we look down at them. A lot. When we do this, we don't see the world around us. I am guilty of this as well. There are so many incredible ways we can use this technology to complete tasks, connect, and learn. But I believe the way we truly connect is by looking up. We share a smile. We pause and ask a question. We linger. We engage in a conversation. We relate.

Retaining. At the same time, we work hard to retain the relationships we have. Quarantine and isolation during the pandemic made this more difficult than ever before. Facetime and zoom helped us stay connected when we couldn't physically be together. Effort is required here; much like watering plants, relationships won't continue and grow without feeding them. To retain important relationships in my life, I work to do the following:

★ Daily text into our family group chat to tell everyone I love them with a reminder to be awesome in every way they can. I include the occasional memes, funny pictures, motivational quotes, and news we are all interested in.
★ Weekly phone call to my sister with text messages throughout the week
★ Sending to some of my close teacher friends funny memes and pictures that only other educators can understand
★ Reaching out on holidays to send friends good wishes, even when I don't celebrate that particular holiday
★ Organizing a block party with neighbors
★ Volunteering at school when I can to support students, families, and our administration with initiatives throughout the school year

> ★ Phone calls and text messages to each of my parents, who are in their 70s and 80s
> ★ Remembering my students' favorite video games/sports teams/hobbies/interests and asking about them on a regular basis
> ★ Positive comments and likes on friends' news about their children and their lives on social media
> ★ Responding to text messages promptly
> ★ Sharing resources for educators on social media
> ★ Scheduling get-togethers with good friends
> ★ Asking people how they are doing first, before I talk about myself or my family and listening with intention while I hear what's going on
> ★ Sending a comprehensive weekly newsletter to my students' families, filled with smiling pictures of their children from our week of learning and growing together, information about what we learned and did and useful resources for parents as well as about myself and my family; I use Adobe Spark for this purpose.
> ★ Posting pictures and information on Class Dojo about what is going on in our classroom and our school for families
> ★ Giving compliments to family, friends, students, co-workers, neighbors, and retail employees

While all of this takes time and effort, it is well worth it! The reward is the continuing connections with others.

Offboarding. At the same time, we have to get rid of relationships that no longer make sense. This can be an emotional or even heartbreaking process, but it's a necessary one. When relationships become confusing or are out of balance and we are giving more than we receive or when we experience pain at the hands of a relationship, we may need to let go. This is a painful process. I've had to say a quiet goodbye to relationships that just withered over time or became too painful, confusing, or toxic to enjoy. When a relationship that is supposed to be helpful and joyful starts to shrink my Box of Energy with no upside, I know it's time to say goodbye. It can be painful or liberating. We need to be aware of the signs that we may need to offboard a relationship and be brave enough to do so. With some, this can be especially difficult.

2020 changed everything for us. Every single person on the planet was impacted by Covid-19, some much more than others. Racial injustices were on display. Uncertainty and anxiety increased. People felt deeply about all of this. Many people changed. They grew and evolved. Some reconsidered their moral values and stance on issues. Some recommitted to what they already believed. But many, many people changed. In light of this, many relationships blossomed and some withered. I think this is natural. We walk through many stages in life. When I start to develop the uncomfortable feeling that perhaps a relationship is not right for me or that it's no longer working, I ask myself these questions:

Do I spend time with this person? If so, how often and what kind of time is it? My sister Tracy wisely remarked recently, "friends spend time together". How true this is. The way we spend time together may grow, evolve, and change, but true connection is felt when we carve out the time to relate. What could have previously been time together in person could now be time together texting on the phone or Facetime. But it's still time that reflects care and effort. Some relationships may fade when we don't feed them with regular time together. You'll know when a change occurs; you'll miss the person and the togetherness, the laughter, and the relating. You'll have great memories but they won't be enough. Friends who live far away differ from those nearby. I have friends that I feel much closer to who are distant physically compared with some nearby where the connection has trailed off. Reflection will help you determine if something is newly missing and an adjustment needs to be made.

Are we both feeding the relationship with an equal level of effort? If not, is there a reason why that makes sense? Relationships are like a recipe. They have different ingredients and in the case of human connection, contributions are needed from everyone involved. When contributions are balanced, we feel this in a wonderful way. We can enjoy the satisfaction as well as the positive impact of the effort we put out and the benefits we receive from the other. There are times when things may not be in balance. If one friend or family member is going through a difficult time, we can support them as needed during an illness, a transition, or a loss. But if the equation is out of balance for no discernable reason and we find ourselves making most or all of the connection effort, something is probably off. If text messages are not returned and offers to get together either are ignored or are routinely declined, it's time to think deeply about the relationship. Again, reflecting deeply can help us identify when something is amiss, and it may be time to reassess a relationship.

Is this relationship making me feel confused, angry, or sad? This is such a simple question that powerfully reveals when something may be off in a relationship. Sometimes, the other may want the relationship to continue, but only on their terms. This puts the relationship out of balance. Efforts to connect and invitations to spend time together that are not accepted are a clear sign. You can take care of yourself by recognizing and acting on these signs. Toxic words may be spoken or written; this is hurtful and can be hard to recover from. Time spent together may grow uncomfortable if topics of conversation include gossip or speaking negatively about others in the community or other people's children. Of course, I don't want previously good relationships to be over, but I may have to face the fact that continuing to try to make these relationships work is taking up valuable and precious space in my Box of Energy. If I find I am often confused or uncomfortable about where I stand in the relationships and this causes me sadness, I have to look out for myself and ask hard questions about continuing the connection. Again, deep reflection, though painful at times, can be helpful in determining a path forward.

Overall, offboarding can be difficult. It can also be a relief. When we consider offboarding relationships, we need to do it with clarity and also do it carefully. As we extract ourselves from connections that no longer work, it may be painful for the other party as well. Losing connections can hurt. Show yourself love and grace in this process.

Wondering. Finally, as living, breathing, evolving human beings, we can wonder about our relationships. We can wonder if they still make sense, if they support our core values, if they are helpful or hurtful, or if we are benefiting someone else with our presence. When a relationship causes me confusion or pain, I start to deeply wonder about it and ask myself the questions above to help me make sense of the connection and evaluate whether or not it's still working.

We can also view our relationships with wonder. I like to think about taking a bird's-eye view of ourselves with our friends, colleagues, neighbors, and families as we relate to, and with, them while we live our lives. If we were to look down on a conversation or a moment, would it make sense to us? If it did, would it fill us with wonder and awe, the way a magical relationship in a movie might? It's worth thinking about. And when it does, it's worth noticing and savoring when it's good.

Each relationship we have is a connection. It can be deep and wide or slim and fleeting. But at the heart of any relationship is the connection we share. Much like we can in our everyday lives, when we see and notice the small things we experience, we can see, notice, and savor the small connections we encounter. A fleeting, even microscopic, connection can be powerful. I experienced this when I was on my way to the airport to fly to South Africa in 2019 as Global Learning Fellow with the NEA Foundation. I relayed this experience to a friend who was creating a blog series on human connection in the early days of the pandemic in April 2020. Here is my recollection of a fleeting but powerful moment as written in "The Human Connection Chronicles", a collection of essays curated by a friend named Katie. At this moment, I savored every second of this fleeting connection. Here is this story, as recalled on April 17, 2020.

> **Story #3: A Car // A Conversation // A Connection**
>
> "Nerves alive, excitement coursing through my veins, I waited at the end of our driveway. My Uber would be there in 7 minutes. 7 minutes. I just had to get through 7 minutes before I embarked on the first leg of a momentous journey I had been preparing to take for over a year.
>
> South Africa. It's not every day that a teacher from Wilmington, Delaware travels to South Africa. Always a traveler at heart, I was ecstatic; the day had finally arrived. In my mind, I turned over the moment a year earlier when I learned I had been awarded a Global Learning Fellowship by the NEA Foundation that would culminate in this trip.
>
> I had not traveled out of the country in years. Life just didn't allow it recently. We had kids, careers, bills, and responsibilities. We knew we wanted to do some international travel before our oldest left for college and certainly in retirement, but not now.
>
> I thought back to my journeys over the years, trips to three continents other than North America. Australia with friends to celebrate our 30th birthdays. The Harbour Bridge Climb in Sydney. Snorkeling at the Great Barrier Reef. South America and Europe for work while I was an auditor for The Walt Disney Company. Visiting Iguazu Falls at the point where Brazil and Argentina meet. Strolling through Colonia, a small lovely town, in Uruguay. Paris Cafés. London Pubs. A James Joyce walking tour in Dublin. Skiing in Quebec in high school. Sun in Mexico for Spring Break in college. It had been so long. This moment was special.
>
> My Uber pulled up and a friendly driver got out to help me with my bag. It was a sunny day in July, the ride peaceful and calm. My mind was racing with excitement, thoughts of the long journey did not worry me, I had my eye on the prize at the end of the trip: Cape Town in South Africa. The driver asked me where I was going. I answered politely. Normally I do not engage in much small talk on planes or trains, in cabs or cars. I just don't. Being an elementary school teacher has taught me I need to conserve my energy when I don't have to expend it. Being social, all day, every day, with over 20 young children during the school year is a lot. I am good at it, but at times I climb inside myself, posing as an introvert, to recover.

The driver's lilting accent caught my attention. The lovely cadence of his words immediately made me want to answer! I explained my journey, proudly explaining that I was on my way to my fifth continent, joining teachers from around the country. He asked what I was looking forward to the most; I answered: schools. I couldn't wait to see what schools were like in South Africa: the learners, the teachers, how they looked and sounded, lunch and breakfast foods, daily routines, their place in society.

He shared that he was from a small village in Kenya. His school had been just a few rooms in his town without electricity. He loved it, though, and said his teachers in elementary school were kind and hardworking, helping the kids to see beyond the current moment in their lives to look for more. I loved his words and his story. I asked him more about his life, his experience in the United States and his family.

He shared his ideal setup. Kenya, warmest during our winter months, was where he returned every year to spend time with his family after the summer travel season in the US. He had the best of both worlds, loving being a driver during the warmer months in the US when people traveled more often and going home to good weather with savings to see the people he loved. As I turn this conversation over in my mind, I wish I remembered his name.

We pulled up to the Philadelphia airport. I smiled. My driver was amiable and so lovely. He helped me with my bag. It was the perfect way to spend my journey to the airport, the minutes whizzing by as we chatted. He was a natural conversationalist. Was he put in my path? I am sure of it. Were higher forces at work? Maybe. Maybe not. I am grateful to whoever or whatever sent me a lovely human from the continent of Africa, my destination, to bathe the first part of my journey in light, kindness, and conversation. I prefer to think of it as a lovely gift.

Our connection was simple. Both travelers on the journey of life. Both sharing our story. Both speaking. And both listening. Both smiling. I looked back in my Uber app as I wrote this. His name was Joseph. Joseph was highly rated by everyone he drove.

"Thank you for telling me all about beautiful Kenya!"

"Joseph was kind and very professional. Thank you, Joseph."

"Thank you for helping me help my store!!"

"Sorry I didn't have a lot of money on my Uber card would have gave you more."

And my favorite: "French fries!"

That day, in that car ride, Joseph from Kenya and I connected. In the car. With a conversation. Connection was born and it remains with me today. I am grateful."

Be sure to look out for and notice those small, powerful, and fleeting connections that can mean so much. Reflecting on this experience now, years later, is bringing me back to that moment in the most delightful of ways. I noticed, savored, and shared it in a way that allows me to go back to it. I am so glad I did. You can see the full, original piece here.

TABLE 6.3 Link and QR code for "Story #3: A Car, a Conversation, a Connection"

Resource	Link to Access	QR Code to Access
Human Connection Blog: "*Story #3: A Car, a Conversation, a Connection*"	https://bit.ly/EASELcar	

Proactive Strategies for Developing Relationship Skills

Just like we practice when we learn how to ride a bike, we can practice developing and honing our skills around relationships. This is work in the Confidence Zone of SEL. We can try out skills and strategies and see what works best for us. Very powerful ideas relate to the skill of listening well.

Learn How to be a Good Listener. A few years ago, I was looking for some resources to use in the first weeks of school with my students to teach them about and practice SEL. I found a gem I still treasure! One of my favorite resources about relationships is a video made by fourth-grade kids on YouTube 10 years ago. It is one minute and 36 seconds long, and as with so many other things, it stopped me cold in my tracks. A gold nugget buried deep in the internet, this video shows a group of fourth graders giving incredible advice to help us become good listeners, naming listening as "an important life skill". Here are the ideas from the video.

Eye contact. It's so hard to make eye contact! I know this because I struggle with it myself. When I teach kids to do it, they find it really uncomfortable and struggle with it because they are just not used to doing it! However, making eye contact is a simple and powerful way to see someone and signal that you are listening to them and that you care enough to do so, even in difficult conversations. With practice we can get better at it.

Patience. This is also a tough one for me. As a general task master, I am constantly thinking about what I have to get done, what is still on my mental to-do list, and what is generally on my mind, including what worries me. I want to move onto the next thing. Slowing down and being patient and actually practicing being patient help me to get better at it. The best practice for me comes when I need to listen to someone who speaks slowly, such as one of my students. I have come to appreciate someone who takes their time articulating thoughts, stories, and ideas more slowly than I would.

Interrupting. Can you remember a time recently when you were interrupted? I can. It's not fun! It's really annoying to have someone cut you off in mid-thought or mid-story before you can finish your thoughts. Recalling just how awful I feel when I am interrupted helps me to avoid doing it when I am speaking with someone else. I have to work very hard at this.

Questions. This goes back to my husband's simple advice around socializing. People love to be asked questions; this can really help to form connections. This can also help with attentiveness and patience, as questions lay the path for continuing a conversation and engaging in a back-and-forth exchange. Relating this back to my own personal experience, thinking how I feel when someone asks me questions (which is quite good!), reminds me to do this in conversations.

Staying on topic. Whenever someone quickly and randomly changes the subject in a conversation, I get confused. This may also make me want to end a conversation. By relating to the topic and asking appropriate follow-up questions, we can signal that we care about the person we are listening to and what they are saying. This helps us form connections.

Body language. If we fold our arms, frown, and look away, we signal that we don't want to be in a conversation, which signals a lack of caring about the person we are relating to. Relaxed body posture, smiles, and nodding can help with the connection we are having as we listen. This can also help us stay focused on the person we are talking to and the words we are hearing.

Distractions. This might be one of the hardest ideas to embrace today. Notifications, alarms, text messages, emails, smart watches, and alerts from various sources distract us. A great practice for me is making sure my phone is away when I am listening. I turn it over, place it out of reach, or put it away in my bag when I need to be fully present to listen. It's a challenge but it can be done with mindful practice and effort and then it becomes second nature.

Open-mindedness. We all have our ideas about various topics: the way the world should work, how kids should act, the best vacation spot. The list goes on. We learn and grow when we consider other thoughts, perspectives, and everyday ideas. This is how solutions can be born, how innovative ideas can be shared, and how people expand their thinking. Being open-minded helps us learn and grow.

Empathy. Brené Brown tells us that an empathetic response never begins with "At least ..." when listening to someone share a problem or pain. A simple example of this could be when someone is upset because their team experiences a tough loss and someone else says "At least you won last week," which doesn't validate the emotions and loss they are having in the present moment. I am often guilty of using this phrase, particularly with my own children, when they are going through something difficult. I work now to nod and listen and be present when someone is sharing pain, and I avoid saying "At least ...".

The power of recall. This is so hard for me! At times, I find myself forgetting what someone just told me. When this happens, I know I have not been listening; it's powerful proof. To help with this, I silently repeat names to myself or bits and pieces of information, such as where someone works or where they live, after I hear them. I am getting better at this and know how great someone feels when you remember some small detail and bring it up in the next conversation.

You can watch the entire video here.

TABLE 6.4 Link and QR code to "How to Listen Well"

Resource	Link to Access	QR Code to Access
Video: "*How To Be a Good Listener*"	https://bit.ly/EASELlisten	

Learn about holidays and cultural celebrations beyond your own. We are all experts on our own traditions and celebrations. We know when they will arrive on the calendar, how to say them correctly, what to do when they occur, and how to greet others on the particular day. Most of us can get better at understanding cultural celebrations and holidays that fall outside of our traditions, so that we can offer greetings to our friends, neighbors, co-workers, and students who come from and celebrate cultures and religions different from ours. I have been so fortunate to be an educator, as in classrooms we see many faiths and backgrounds come together in one community. I love this! I have truly enjoyed learning about various traditions and celebrations. So many of them have great commonalities such as fireworks, festive food, worship, preparation, gatherings with loved ones, and gratitude.

Some are solemn, some are joyful. They are all important. I know more about various celebrations than I did five years ago, and I am so thankful for this new knowledge. In my own life, I can use specific language and expressions when I offer a greeting to a friend or student who is celebrating a holiday that I do not. In the classroom, I ask students to share their traditions with our community and they love doing this! This builds confidence, connection, and social awareness among all of us. With curiosity and the internet at hand, this is a simple and fun process.

Pay attention to current events. At any given time, we know that current events happening around the world are impacting people all over the globe, both positively and negatively. When we work to notice what is happening in the world, we can become aware of when something happening may impact a friend and we can offer support if needed. I'll never forget the day in my classroom when almost half of my class came in and put on red and yellow bracelets. It seemed to be a regular morning in Delaware. During our morning check-in, students shared that they were sad, scared, stressed, and worried about a hurricane that was happening in Florida. One student had a parent on a business trip in Florida. Others had just seen the news coverage of the storm and were stressed. We took some time to talk about our feelings that day and also look at a map so students understood that it was unlikely the hurricane would impact us. When senseless things happen in the world, they impact us deeply, children more so at times. If an act of violence occurs against a certain racial group, we can notice that and be mindful of our interactions with friends and neighbors who share the same race as those impacted. This includes our postings on social media as well as our words and actions. When a storm hits a particular geographic area, we can check in with friends who are nearby and make sure they are OK. This is a relatively easy way to show friends, loved ones, and the members of the communities where we live and work that we care. Care supports positive relationships.

In-the-Moment Strategies to Support Relationships

Be nice and show kindness. If we want people to enjoy our company, we need to make them feel good when they are with us. How can we do this? By simply being nice and showing kindness, of course. This works well in relationships where both people are equally contributing to its success and are enjoying each other's time and company. It is likely that niceness, kindness, and compliments will flow naturally into this space. It can be quite a different story when a relationship becomes prickly, uneven, or unpleasant. But it is still a very powerful way to create positive feelings that enable two parties to go forward even when the relationship is difficult. The act of being nice can change the vibe in the room and break up an uncomfortable silence. Occasions when this can be useful or helpful could be with a relative, with the parent of a student who is struggling in school, or with people who have been critical of us. To be quite honest, it can be disarming at times and help to relieve tension so that a conversation can go forward. I know that when I am nice and compliment someone I'm struggling to connect to, I just feel better having embraced kindness as a tool to move through something challenging, such as a difficult conversation.

The next time a student is giving you a hard time, think about just being nice and giving them a compliment. It's disarming. A student might look at you with confusion. Smile back at them. It changes the feel of the room. It might just diffuse tension and create the good vibes needed to move forward. I know how great I feel when someone is nice to me and compliments my shoes, hair, outfit, energy, lesson, earrings, or teaching skills. It lifts me up and helps me move forward. I want to create that feeling in others, so showing kindness and being nice have become powerful tools for me in developing and maintaining relationships. Practicing kindness also has mental benefits for us, as I explored in Chapter 4, so it's a win-win for everyone.

There are a few ways this idea comes alive in my classroom. They are projects and traditions that have been part of our classroom culture for years.

★ **The birthday tradition**. We all want our birthday to be a day we enjoy, and we all want to feel special and celebrated. Years ago, I created a special ritual for birthdays in our classroom. On each person's birthday, including mine, we all share what we like best about the birthday person. We sit or stand in a circle and someone volunteers to go first and share what they love about the birthday person. I teach students to look directly at the person they are celebrating, and they say something like "Remy, what I like best about you is that you have a great smile". Everyone shares an idea. No one can pass. People can share the same idea as someone else if they would like to. If people need time to think, they get it. I have seen kids come up with the most amazing and caring ideas to share, such as what I like best about you is "you have great headbands", "you're always on time", or "you're a great friend". One of the most special sentiments I heard about me from a student was when one said: "Mrs. Turner, what I like best about you is that when we do something bad, you don't give up on us. You help us get better and you forgive us".

You can bring this wonderful tradition to your family at home or your next staff meeting. I have had to do this on the first day of school, and even then, they get it right after I model it. I think because at the heart of it is the joy we receive when we treat others well and the hope that we'll get to feel this special on our birthday. This also helps with relationships that don't always work well. Differences are set aside and grudges are forgotten while we engage in this task. I always invite a family member to come in for the tradition; they love it and also share with the group what they love best about their child. It's simply the best!

I did a version of this at home with my husband Dan for his 50th birthday. We had a big party and I set up a table with pens and index cards so everyone could share "what they like best about Dan". We read them out at the party; it was sweet, fun, and emotional, and I still have the cards as a keepsake of a special occasion. When I asked Dan if it was OK to include these sentiments in this book, he said sure. Then he looked back at the pictures of the cards people had written over five years ago and he got a smile on his face. This just reminds me of the positive power of letting people know what we like best about them. Who wouldn't enjoy that? You can see some of the lovely sentiments our friends and family shared about Dan here.

★ **The Compliment Project**. I started this idea when I was teaching second grade online in 2021. It was winter and I felt we needed something fun in the new year that would create a great vibe. So each day for a week, we celebrated five different students and every person gave them a compliment. By the end of the week, each student had received over 20 compliments. Since we were online, we posted sticky-note compliments on Google Jamboard. It was an instant hit! The receivers of the compliments simply glowed with happiness when they got their compliments. I downloaded each Jamboard as an image and sent it to the student in our Education Management System, Schoology, and I also emailed a copy to the student's family so they could see all of the wonderful things that others thought about their child.

Now we do this with sticky notes on chart paper or put the sticky notes into a box for the complimented person to enjoy later. However you set it up, it is solid gold! There are smiles everywhere and sometimes people can't stop giving the compliments; they want to give more than one. I have also done this activity with college students and it works just as well. With all ages, when we work in pairs, I ask each person to give their partner a compliment before we do the academic task. It seems no matter how old someone is or what the situation is, people can't get enough compliments and they love the great vibes generated when others are nice to them. They are happy to participate as well.

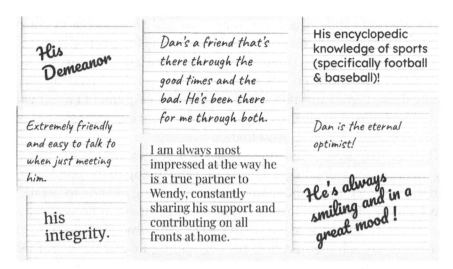

Figure 6.3 Birthday tradition: What we love best about Dan.

Compromise. We have all been here before, in a difficult space where we need to figure out what comes next, locked in disagreement. Staying in this space and taking resources we could use to manage ourselves and using them on disagreement will deplete our Box of Energy more quickly than if we compromise. That's a somewhat clinical way to think about it, but I find it to be true. So, in difficult moments when I don't want to compromise, I have to ask myself: is this worth it? Does it help to stay locked in a battle, putting my foot down? What would happen if I proposed a compromise that would move us forward? It might strengthen the relationship. It might save it. It will certainly leave me with more energy for other tasks, problems, and ideas I need to take care of and consider. Sometimes when a compromise might work is in an everyday situation where family members are deciding what to watch on TV or eat for dinner. In professional settings, we can let colleagues set agendas, choose a lunch spot, schedule a meeting time, or go first. It's that simple. To help me, I think about my Box of Energy and I remind myself how much energy it takes to dig in my heels on something and save that for really important situations that may have to do with money, our children, what's best for kids at school, important family matters, and health and mental wellness. I remember that I actually feel better when I compromise than when I don't. It's another simple but powerful tool in the skill set we need to establish and maintain relationships.

Slow down. I love our son so much. He is funny, creative, intelligent, strong, and highly entertaining. And he also knows how to push everyone's buttons. He can annoy you in the blink of an eye or create a disagreement or argument over the most benign thing, and before you know it you are down the rabbit hole, really frustrated and maybe even downright angry about something that doesn't even matter! He would make an amazing lawyer someday with his ability to draw things out and trap people in conversation, mincing words and creating frustration. I am getting better at seeing this coming, understanding what our son's triggers are, and also reading signals around when I should even talk to him. But when I don't read signals well or ignore them, there I am right in the middle of an argument I don't want to have and probably don't even really care about. I am expending my precious energy on something that doesn't matter.

When this happens, I slow down. There are several ways to do this. Some of my favorites are going to get a drink of water, going to the bathroom, saying I need to switch the laundry to the dryer, or going outside to get the mail or checking my phone and texting my sister. All of these options allow me to momentarily leave the space we are in and this is extremely helpful in giving me a minute to cool down, collect myself, and figure out the path forward. When I can't leave the space, such as when we are in the car or out somewhere, I find a place to look at and fix my gaze there and count. Or I turn up the music. This helps me focus on something else instead of my feelings or my next clever remark.

I also use this strategy successfully in my classroom. In the back of the classroom, high up on the wall there is a homemade sign that says "See the Good, Be the Good". When I need to, I look there and breathe. I also utilize a strategy of giving my students a 3- to 5-minute brain break when I'm actually the one that needs the break. Yes, you read that correctly! When I need a brain break or a moment to collect myself, I give my students a brain break. A brain break will never hurt a group of students, and when I need to disrupt my dysregulation process, this helps me to do so. This is clearly tied to my self-management practice as well. As I recognize the physical and emotional signs of my frustration, I can do something about it before I completely lose my cool. Students have calming spaces and ways to take breaks and timeouts when needed. Teachers do not. So we have to create our own ways to cope with difficult situations and tough relationship moments as they happen. Slowing down helps me do this both at home and in my professional setting.

Reflective Strategies to Support Relationships

When a relationship is not going well, I use reflection to think deeply about it and to try to figure out what is going on. One of my favorite ways to embrace this thinking is to compare and contrast some of my relationships to really dig into what is going on with them. When I analyze various relationships that are going well and compare them with those that are not, identifying specifically what I do and say, it's pretty easy to see what is going on. Here is some of my analysis.

Relationship Skills Matter ◆ 143

Compare & Contrast Your Relationships

- My relationship with my sibling is not working.

  I give unsolicited advice. A lot.

- My relationship with one of my co-workers is not working.

  I am judging them.

- My relationship with my boss is working well.

  I am kind to them and listen well.

- My relationship with one of my friends is working.

  I check in with them on a regular basis and we make plans to connect.

- My relationship with my child is working.

  We spend time doing fun things together. I listen well and empathize.

Figure 6.4 Comparing and contrasting relationships.

A few big ideas emerge from this process. I need to listen well in a way that enables people to know and understand I am listening to them. I have to stay out of judgment. It's just an inefficient use of resources, the kind that shrinks my Box of Energy and also doesn't make anyone feel good. I need to avoid giving advice when it's not asked for. Then I need to focus on what works. It's everything we have been learning about in this chapter that we can do proactively and in the moment to support connection: be nice, use empathy, make an effort to check in and connect, spend time together, and then notice and savor those experiences to feed connection and positivity going forward. It's almost like a formula with ingredients that are required or that should never be added. It just makes sense. This window of my classroom shares the important reminder that kindness and empathy matter in relationships.

Figure 6.5 Classroom window.

I have not dissected every aspect of Casel's definition of relationship skills here. The focus has been on personal relationships and what we can do, or perhaps should not do, to feed them and make them successful as well as on applications of these ideas in our professional settings. We've also talked about how to know when it's time to let go of a relationship. All of this work and these ideas cascade down into our classroom when we embrace and live them. If we're successful with relationships outside of our learning spaces and view our students with the same importance as our personal connections, we'll have successful relationships with them as well. For us, it's helpful to use these strategies in all aspects of our lives instead of just parts of them selectively. This is part of our authentic SEL growth. It doesn't happen in just one place, some of the time; it's a part of who we are and how we are. When we embrace this holistic approach, we benefit in so many ways.

Figure 6.6 Building up our SEL skills. Created by the author on Google Jamboard.

 Reflection Questions

It's time to reflect on and process the information we are learning. Feel free to go back into the chapter to dig into some of these ideas. You can answer these questions by thinking about them, recording ideas in a journal, adding notes here, or creating audio or video notes.

TABLE 6.5 Link and QR code for the online reflection journal

\multicolumn{3}{l}{*I created an online tool with Google Jamboard that you can also access and use on your own if you'd like to. You can access it below. When you access the file, you'll be asked if you want to make a copy of the file. Say "yes" and this file will be in your Google Drive for you to use and refer back to throughout your reading of the text.*}
Resource	**Link to Access**	**QR Code to Access**
"Embracing Adult SEL" Google Jamboard Reflection Journal	https://bit.ly/EASELjournal5-8	

TABLE 6.6 Reflection activity: Relationship skills

Share at least three ideas about relationship skills.		
Idea #1	**Idea #2**	**Idea #3**

TABLE 6.7 Reflection activity: Listening skills

\multicolumn{3}{l	}{*Listening well is an important life skill. Identify three strategies you can use to become a good listener and explain why they are important.*}
Strategy #1	**Strategy #2**	**Strategy #3**
What?	What?	What?
Why?	Why?	Why?

TABLE 6.8 Holidays and celebrations

\multicolumn{3}{l	}{*Learn about three holidays and cultural celebrations that are outside of your traditions. Consider these questions: What are they called? When are they celebrated? Who celebrates them? What traditions are involved?*}
Celebration 1	**Celebration 2**	**Celebration 3**
What?	What?	What?
When?	When?	When?
Who?	Who?	Who?
How?	How?	How?

TABLE 6.9 Reflection activity: Compare and contrast relationships

Compare and contrast a relationship working well and one that is not. Identify the things you do and say that have led the relationships to where they are today.
Relationship working well
What do you do?
What do you say?
Relationship not working well
What do you do?
What do you say?

TABLE 6.10 Reflection activity: In-the-moment strategies for relationships

In-the-moment strategies that support positive relationships include being nice, slowing down, and compromising. Give an example of each strategy you can demonstrate in your own life.		
Being nice	Compromising	Slowing down

7

Synthesizing Your SEL Skills
Powerful Decision-Making

"Are you OK?"

There it was. That same question was posed to me by several colleagues in one week. I always said yes. Deep down inside, I knew I was generally OK, far from crisis or unmanageable despair. But I was struggling. I activated my self-awareness and started to think about why people were asking me this question instead of the usual "How are you?" or "What's up?"

It was early 2022, my third year of pandemic teaching, and I was burning out. This question was a key indicator. I knew it meant that I didn't look and sound OK to my colleagues, that something was off, and that I was different. I also knew this was the case. I could feel a change happening that was not for the better. Throughout the 12 years I worked at my school, I had been hard-working and helpful most of the time. I invested a lot in my students and families and worked tirelessly to create an engaging and enjoyable learning environment and experience for our students. I contributed to the entire school community as well. With others, I fostered school-wide programs such as "Girls on the Run" (a character-building program that inspires girls to recognize their strengths and build connections while training to run a 5k race), a hands-on school garden, and established a community recycling event. I volunteered at school events when needed and donated my time in the form of providing professional development to our staff as well as district employees. When people started asking me this question more often, I had little energy to do such things anymore as I felt depleted, and just getting through each day teaching had become an arduous task. Students had returned to school in the fall of 2021 with enormous academic and social needs due to the pandemic, and it was taking a toll. All of us had a smaller window of tolerance for stress. Worst of all, I was starting to lose the joy I usually felt in my job. So what was going on?

Deep inside, I knew something was changing, and I was devastated to face that fact but I had to. I was burning out. When school closed in March 2020, it was difficult to figure out how to continue on when so many things were uncertain and we really didn't even know how to do our jobs. Even so, I never thought about leaving my job. The fall of 2020 brought remote learning and additional stresses and challenges around procedures, health and safety, and teaching online. In a way, there was a lot of excitement around developing and trying new skills and strategies with a growth mindset. So once again, even though things were difficult, I never wanted to leave my job. It was somewhat of a relief when the school year ended in June 2021, and I was excited for the chance to recover, recharge, and get ready, hopefully, for normalcy the following fall. I still never considered leaving my job.

The fall of 2022 arrived and I was so excited to get back to the classroom! But I didn't have an understanding of how great student needs would be when school began. As the fall progressed, it was becoming clear that students seemed to be one or two years behind their physical age in both their academic and social emotional development. Returning to a five-day school week with regular hours was a significant challenge for everyone. Students constantly asked me why we went to school every day and why school lasted until after 3 p.m. when the year before students had an asynchronous day every Wednesday and school ended at 2 p.m. Inside, I was asking myself the same questions.

The year continued on, and in the early months of 2022, I found myself thinking about leaving my job and the teaching profession. This devastated me inside, but I knew it was a very real and different feeling that I had to deeply examine and address. I was at an inflection point and I had to make a very important decision. My self-awareness was kicking in and telling me I really needed to pay attention to my feelings.

To me, responsible decision-making is the synthesis of the other core social emotional learning (SEL) skills we have examined so far. I truly don't see how we can make responsible decisions that will help us in life if we don't know ourselves deeply (self-awareness), recognize and work through how we feel when we experience significant emotions (self-management), and understand others as well as what's happening in the world around us (social awareness). Strong, trusted relationships give us someone to lean on when we need it (relationship skills) and that includes decision-making time.

So there I was at this inflection point, 12 years into my second career, a wife and the mom of two teenagers, living in the wake of a global pandemic, trying to figure out if I should still be a teacher. I knew many educators were experiencing significant burnout and some were leaving the profession. This was all over the news and social media and in the local community. I knew my job had gotten harder in multiple ways. And I knew that people around me were recognizing that I was different – and perhaps not for the better. There were lots of signs that I had to really think about where I was and where I was going. With my SEL skill growth over the previous few years, I knew I had to do a few things to help me make an important decision in a responsible way.

> ★ I had to talk to people whom I trusted and who knew me well. This, of course, is my consiglieri in life, my husband Dan. He could see me struggling. He encouraged me to look into different options that might be a good fit and could reduce my workload. I also talked to a few trusted educator friends to share my struggle. They could relate over how difficult our jobs had become. They immediately heard and validated me, reminding me that I would likely have some good options given my experience, awards and recognition, and positive relationships in the community. Every single person I spoke to validated what I was thinking. They knew me well. They could see me struggling. They also had a lot of the same feelings. They understood where I was and they were supportive. I was enormously grateful to each and every one of them. My relationship skills helped me to sustain all of those connections, and people were there for me when I needed them to be.
> ★ I thought about other options to pursue when I was regulated and rested. I arrived home each afternoon in such a state of depletion, I couldn't do much. As I am a true morning person, I save all of my mental heavy lifting for the early hours of the day. So I would do research on other jobs, apply to other jobs, and think about the entire situation as part of my morning routine or on the weekends when I had the bandwidth and energy to devote to it. My strong self-awareness and commitment to self-management helped me to do this.
> ★ My social awareness helped me to understand that many educators were facing the same situation as myself. It validated my thinking and told me it was OK for me to feel that way. I committed to myself that I would finish the school year in as strong a way as I possibly could. Leaving in the middle of the year was not an option I wanted to explore; it would be devastating to students and families and would have a negative impact on some of my relationships.

I began a long process of looking for and applying for the right job. Although it was difficult to decide to leave, I immediately felt relief and empowerment once I made that decision. It started me on a path to a future I could see. It was making a responsible decision.

Defining Responsible Decision-Making

Once again, let's see what the dictionary says about the components of this phrase. When we look up responsible, decision, and making, we learn the following.

TABLE 7.1 Definitions of responsible, decision, and making

Responsible	Able **to choose for oneself** between **right** and wrong
Decision	A determination arrived at **after consideration**
Making	The act or **process of** forming, causing, **doing**, or coming into

From these meanings, we can put together a definition that might sound something like this: responsible decision-making is the "process of choosing for oneself a determination that can be considered right." Of course, what is right for one person may not be ideal for another. The word "right" here is a subjective one; make sure it is personal to you.

Casel defines responsible decision-making as

"the abilities to make caring and constructive choices about personal behavior and social interactions across diverse situations. This includes the capacities to consider ethical standards and safety concerns, and to evaluate the benefits and consequences of various actions for personal, social, and collective well-being."

Key concepts that are part of the definition include

"demonstrating curiosity and open-mindedness, learning how to make a reasoned judgment after analyzing information, data, and facts, identifying solutions for personal and social problems, anticipating and evaluating the consequences of one's actions, recognizing how critical thinking skills are useful both inside and outside of school, reflecting on one's role to promote personal, family, and community well-being and evaluating personal, interpersonal, community, and institutional impacts".

As educators and human beings, we make hundreds of decisions every single day. It can be tiring. In classrooms, our choices can dramatically alter the course of things. At times, it can seem like a boulder is rolling down a hill at high speed after we decide something and we are powerless to stop it. With intentional work, we can get better at making decisions. We'll never decide perfectly. As human beings, we are fraught with imperfection. But we can learn, grow, and evolve as decision-makers. This will once again support SEL growth and development in the Confidence Zone.

Proactive Strategies for Responsible Decision-Making

At the beginning of the pandemic, I partnered with Empatico, an online learning tool that connected students with classrooms around the world. The mission behind this work is to build curiosity, practice kindness, and share connections among students across the globe. It's an incredible organization with great people. They contacted me because they knew educators were struggling and they wanted to create something that would be supportive. When they contacted me in late March 2020 about building a professional development experience in the form of a live webinar, I almost declined. I was completely overwhelmed by the early days of the pandemic and mentally exhausted even though we were spending all of our time at home! But I thought again, and in my desire to help others, I said yes.

As we started to plan, we considered various formats and settled on a one-hour live webinar that would also be recorded and eventually shared. We wanted to see and validate all of the feelings that everyone was having, particularly educators. We had some good ideas but were getting stuck in the weeds, and I knew the presentation we were putting together needed work. This is where I first worked to create something that was organized around the Casel SEL competency model. Embracing this approach helped us to get organized, and we were able to put together a helpful resource. The Empatico "Empathy Hour" succeeded. The idea was to "offer a space for educators, parents, and caregivers to come together through a virtual meetup to stay connected, find a sense of community, and support one another through trying times". The response was overwhelmingly positive.

If you are interested, you can watch the full Empathy Hour here.

TABLE 7.2 Link and QR code for "Empatico Empathy Hour with Wendy Turner"

Resource	Link to Access	QR Code to Access
Video: *"Empatico Empathy Hour with Wendy Turner"*	https://bit.ly/EASELemp	

I continued to develop a deep understanding of the Casel competency model and have since used this approach in writing and creating learning opportunities for adults. My expertise has since been shared in many blogs, podcasts, and interviews. That small moment, that key decision I made at that time, was a great one! After consideration, I arrived at the point of a determination that was right for me and the world. I said yes to a project that pushed me to grow in a difficult time, created a positive impact, and helped others. It lined up perfectly with my core values of joy, growth, and impact.

When we have the luxury of time as we consider significant, meaningful decisions, there are many ways we can work to make the decisions effectively using specific strategies. These are some of my favorite strategies to help with making good decisions.

Approach decisions with the lens of your core values. Once again, our SEL worlds collide. An important component of our work on self-awareness was to identify our core values. Three of my most important core values are growth, joy, and impact. The act of deciding whether or not to collaborate with Empatico on the Empathy Hour project was an important one for me. At the time, I didn't know it, but this was key. The act of saying yes gave me permission to learn, evolve, and grow during the pandemic while avoiding the stillness and paralysis that were threatening all of us in the early days of Covid-19. Ensuring that you are always equipped with your list of three to five core values will enable you to determine courses of action and paths that are "right" for you when you are faced with a decision point.

Make decisions early in the day. As an early bird with a great degree of self-awareness, I know it is in my best interest to do my most challenging and demanding work early in the day. I can feel my efficiency and energy fade as time passes, and I plan tasks and activities around this. I always thought that if someone were a night owl, the opposite would be true, that we should each do the work that we need to at the time it works for us. Research shows there is a surprising twist with respect to decision-making. According to an analysis of chess game data, decisions that are more accurate and therefore better are made earlier in the day, regardless of whether someone identifies as an early bird or a night owl. The data showed that the most accurate decisions were made between 8 a.m. and 1 p.m. Decisions tended to take longer in the early hours, and as the day went on, decisions were made more quickly but less accurately. We can harness the power of this trend by making important decisions early in the day.

Avoid sunk cost bias. Part of the curse of being really gritty and possessing the ability to persevere is that sometimes when we start something, no matter what, we refuse to abandon it. This is part of sunk cost bias. I first learned about this when I was researching some decision-making tools as part of an Adult SEL training I was putting together. I am so glad I came across this concept because I now work to apply it in my everyday life when I need to and it's quite effective. The idea here is to be able to say no to something when it no longer makes any sense even if you have already put time, effort, and energy into it.

The simplest example from my life is being able to put down a book that I am not enjoying and not being afraid to leave it half read. An avid reader, I am regularly reading more than one book at once. Some I voraciously consume, others I struggle with. If I receive the book as a gift, I find I really want to finish it even though I may not be enjoying it. I go through this thinking process and tell myself that not finishing the book would somehow offend the gift giver, even though they would most likely never even know that I didn't finish the book. I recently put a half-read book back on my shelf and it felt good to do so.

Stated simply, it's making a decision based not on what you have already put into something but on the best course of action. This came into play recently with our son. He had concert tickets that were purchased months in advance. The show was on a weeknight. When it came time for the show, it interfered with his wrestling practice and his team was a top contender for the state championship. He also couldn't find a friend who was able to go, everyone being busy for similar reasons. The concert was in Philadelphia, which would have required one of us to drive him, wait there, and then bring him home late on a school night. We all put our heads together and just decided it wasn't going to work. The tickets were purchased and that money was spent, whether he went or not. It was the right thing to do.

Another example is the piece of clothing that you've never worn and no longer want but that you keep just because you spent money on it in the first place. Wearing something that is no longer in style, that you just don't like, or that doesn't fit is an example of doing something because of some inner guilt around past expense or effort. It won't make us feel good. The money has been spent and that fact won't change whether or not the item is worn. It's OK to part with it. The same can be said for a half-finished project or puzzle. Avoid taxing your Box of Energy just for the sake of finishing something. If it no longer brings you joy, feels like a heavy weight, or is simply something you don't want to do, embrace the decision to abandon it. It's really OK.

Identify pros and cons. This is such a simple strategy. It's almost a cliché. However, I find it incredibly effective to make a physical list of pros and cons around a decision, analyze it, and then use it to make an informed decision. When one side of the list is longer than another, the choice may become very clear. It's also an activity that really engages our critical thinking and forces us to focus deeply on a question. Recently, this worked really well for our daughter. She was accepted to her dream college, however not into the program or location that she wanted. Eventually, the path would lead her to the degree she wanted, but her first year, particularly, would look very different. As someone with diagnosed anxiety, she found herself in a tailspin. When emotions calmed down, she talked it through with her therapist and then made a handwritten list of the pros and cons, eventually deciding to go with the unexpected option and embrace the experience. The list of pros and cons that she shared with all of us was just longer on the pro side. This helped her immeasurably and was such a simple act.

Seek counsel. With big decisions, I need help. I seek out my most trusted advisors when I need them. My consiglieri in life is my husband Dan. He helps me work through situations in a mindful, focused, calm, measured, and clear way. His general demeanor is calm and he communicates in a measured way. I tend to be more impulsive and want to decide things quickly, so his input is enormously helpful. I also regularly seek out advice from my sister Tracy, my parents, and good friends. There is so much value in the perspective of the people we trust, and this goes for decisions in both my personal and professional life. It's a powerful practice to have at the ready that list of people you can go to when needed.

Make decisions when regulated. I am human. There are days when I am not able to think calmly and rationally because I am tired, depleted, annoyed, triggered, sad, and overwhelmed. The most powerful practice I have been able to engage in around this is to become keenly aware of the physical signs of my dysregulation through deep and authentic growth of my self-awareness and to avoid decision-making at those times. This is where self-awareness meets and feeds responsible decision-making. When facing significant decisions, I try to make them when I feel strong, put together, capable, and physically good. I almost never make decisions when I get home from teaching.

I need recovery time. I have to take care of myself so I can take care of others and the rest of my life for the remainder of the day.

Recently, our daughter asked me to look at the website of the college she'll be attending in the fall and help her fill out a form related to orientation and her first-year housing situation. It was 10:10 p.m. I was very close to going to bed, but I told her I would help her with it. As teenagers do, she started scrolling through the web page at what seemed like 10,000 miles per hour. I couldn't follow a thing. My scrolling skills don't hold a candle to our kids' given the amount of time they spend scrolling through TikTok, Instagram, and more. This immediately triggered me because I couldn't follow the information in the form or understand exactly what was being asked, and I started to get really annoyed and eventually yelled at her. Then I felt terrible about doing that! No one wants to be yelled at, particularly before going to bed. I hate yelling but I do it sometimes. So I waited a moment and said: "I'd really like to look at this tomorrow before 9 p.m." She got it and said sure no problem. Then I repaired the situation with an apology and a hug. Finally, I reminded both kids to ask me for what they need before 9 p.m. unless it's an emergency. They got it. They know me. I should have decided to tell my daughter I couldn't help her that late based on how I felt, but I didn't because I wanted to be helpful. Except that I wasn't. It was a reminder for all of us. I don't think we'll make the same mistake again anytime soon.

In-the-Moment Strategies for Responsible Decision-Making

When we are in the middle of a situation, it's hard to slow down and analyze it effectively. When we are in danger, our fight/flight/freeze instincts will take over and hopefully guide us to safety and resolution of a problem. So when we are in the thick of things, it's helpful to have some strategies to help us get through whatever we are facing.

Stop and wait. It happens all the time. I see a situation unfolding and say to myself, I need to intervene, head off a problem before it happens, and fix this. I need to spend energy on it. However, this is not always the case. It can be very helpful to just stop and wait. And by stopping, I mean ceasing physical movement. A few examples come to mind. In a school setting, I see students attempting to work together or play a game at recess. I see things starting to go south – they begin to devolve or not work. Instinctively, I think I need to approach the students and facilitate some type of discussion. But maybe not. I can wait and observe. And I have found that about half of the time, the students work it out. This is great to see! It also saves me from expending energy unnecessarily, thus preserving my Box of Energy, and it also allows them to develop their personal conflict resolution skills. Students need to practice and hone these skills in small, everyday situations. This is the perfect way for them to get better at being successful socially.

Similarly, at home, I can recall situations where this works as well. The morning is always hectic when teenagers can't find their water bottle, car keys, iPad, sneakers, and so on. I can just wait. I can avoid getting upset and yelling. I can be patient and most of the time, with a few moments and a calm parent nearby, they will find what they need and life will go on. And if they don't, life will still go on. When I do this, I stay regulated which leaves me better prepared to support students in the classroom for the day and my Box of Energy stays intact.

Try something different. This is so simple yet so incredibly hard to do. With everyday situations, I find that sometimes I can fall into a predictable one-act play. My part is cast and so are my lines. We all fall into our roles and things play out in a way that we are all familiar with. A powerful practice for me is to try something different. What I usually try is being nice when things are difficult. I mentioned this previously. This works well in both personal and professional settings. When things are going well, we don't have to think hard about what to do next; we are effectively on autopilot. But the moment something is difficult, we are faced with the decision around how to act. We can fall into predictable patterns. When a situation calls for a response, we can try something different. I try to default to being supportive or positive instead of pointing out what is going wrong. When I am late for an appointment and there is traffic, instead of ruminating about it and getting mad, I bring up my favorite album on Spotify in the car or call a friend. When I am waiting a long time in a doctor's office, I use the time to do nothing. It is rare that I am given the time to just sit and think quietly during the day. I do my own type of mindfulness which is just to focus on whatever is in the space: a picture or painting on the wall, a small noise in the soundscape, or some detail around me. It's actually quite nice to be able to give myself permission to not be productive for a time. This ties into both my self-awareness and self-management practices.

Reflective Strategies for Responsible Decision-Making

Once again, my go-to reflective strategy for responsible decision-making is simply to reflect on situations after they occur. It's helpful and revealing to think back and notice both where things went well and where things went awry. In my opinion, this is where all of the SEL competencies meet. I like to ask myself powerful and revealing questions to help me reflect. I often do this as part of my morning routine and my mindfulness practice around my own life. I need a quiet environment and the availability of headspace to process these questions before I expend energy throughout the day, particularly on days I am teaching, which takes so much energy. Weekends away from school are also a great time for me to engage in this work.

Reflective Strategy: Think Back

I succeed at decision-making when:	I fail at decision-making when:
I stay calm	I am emotional
I think about different options	I don't consider options
I think about different perspectives	I don't consider perspectives
I persevere	I give up easily
I am safe and moral	I take the easy way out
I talk to others	I don't seek out help and advice

Figure 7.1 Thinking back on decision-making.

Responsible Decisions I've Made as an Educator

I'll continue to be an imperfect person. I'll have days and situations where I make really good decisions that are sound in many ways and bring about terrific results, and I'll fail miserably on others. But I'll continue to move forward with these skills to improve, and I'll forgive myself when I don't do the best job possible. Over the years, I have already experienced significant growth both personally and professionally. I know you will too. Here are some great decisions I've made as an educator:

> ★ Naming my triggers in the classroom so I can either avoid them or respond in a proactive way that helps me stay regulated.
> ★ Thinking about different parts of the day differently. For instance, when energy dips in the afternoon, I schedule more high-energy learning activities, social learning opportunities, and breaks to help keep us all regulated and on track.
> ★ Embracing and implementing Casel's "3 Signature SEL Practices" in my classroom and professional development sessions as a non-negotiable element of my craft. I'll go into that in detail in Chapter 8.
> ★ Using the word "struggling" to describe what is happening with my students when they are not doing what I need them to do.

For example, I now describe a student who is "misbehaving" as "someone who is struggling to meet behavior expectations". This subtle shift helps me to be more compassionate and then work to uncover what my student needs to be successful and provide them with the support they need.

★ Selecting just three technology tools to embrace in the classroom in 2020 when we pivoted to live, remote learning. I was overwhelmed with all of the options and the training we were doing. Choosing just three tools to embrace and develop expertise with was doable and empowering. This also allowed my students to become extremely proficient with these tools as well. They are Google Jamboard, Microsoft Flip, and Nearpod.

★ Pushing myself to try innovative learning projects such as project-based learning activities or the opportunity to connect with a classroom somewhere outside of Delaware. Taking risks and trying new strategies in the classroom over the years have helped me grow tremendously and have really improved my confidence as an educator.

★ Using time outside of school to think about what I'll do in school. When I am stumped by a problem or challenge with school, I think about it at home or during holiday or vacation time. The best ideas and solutions strike me during a walk with my dog, in the quiet of my morning mindfulness practice, or on a quiet car ride.

★ Committing to be a lifelong learner. I love to read, attend conferences and webinars, try new things, and consume information about different teaching practices, techniques, and approaches. As educators, we can always grow. I have learned so much in this process. In no particular order, here are some of the cherished books I've read that have helped me learn, evolve, and grow as an educator and a human being. What are your favorites?

 ○ *Teach Boldly* by Jennifer Williams
 ○ *Culturally Responsive Teaching & The Brain* by Zaretta Hammond
 ○ *Rest* by Alex Soojung-Kim Pang
 ○ *Fostering Resilient Learners* and *Relationship, Responsibility, and Regulation* by Kristin Souers and Pete Hall
 ○ *Hacking Deficit Thinking* by Dr. Byron McClure and Dr. Kelsie Reed
 ○ *The Light We Carry* by Michelle Obama
 ○ *Building Thinking Classrooms in Mathematics* by Peter Liljedahl
 ○ *Your Teacher Leadership Journey* by Dr. Melissa Collins

160 ◆ Synthesizing Your SEL Skills

- ○ *The PD Book* by Elena Aguilar and Lori Cohen
- ○ *Hacking School Discipline* by Nathan Maynard and Brad Weinstein
- ○ *Think Like Socrates* by Shanna Peeples
- ○ *Mathematical Mindsets* by Jo Boaler
- ○ *The Restorative Journey* by Dr. Malik Muhammad
- ○ *Beyond the Bake Sale* by Anne Henderson, Karen Mapp, Vivian Johnson, and Don Davies
- ○ *The Growth Mindset Coach* by Annie Broke and Heather Hundley
- ○ *Always Strive to Be a Better You* by Pete Hall

Figure 7.2 Some of my favorite books.

A Tough Decision

By now, you may have realized I made the incredibly difficult decision to leave the classroom. I gave notice over the summer and left the school where I had worked for 12 years. It was a complicated feeling, but I felt in my heart and soul that I was doing the right thing, and I knew I needed a change. In the fall, I took a new job that I was incredibly excited about, still in the education profession. However, about six weeks after I started the new job, I realized I had made a mistake. It was a terrific opportunity and a great job surrounded by lovely people, but it was just not right for me.

I was devastated to realize this but had to face the fact that it was not working out. I was making a long commute with an hour drive and sitting at a desk working at a computer for hours on end. Despite being surrounded by very nice people, my physical and mental health were suffering and I knew it. My family also knew this and expressed their concerns. A low point came when my daughter and I were visiting colleges. We were taking a long train ride for the weekend. With so much work to do to keep up with the demands of the job, I purchased a mobile hotspot the night before so I could work on the entire six-hour train ride up and back as well as early in the morning and late at night in our hotel room. I had constant emails asking questions that need responses. At one point on our trip, my daughter looked at me with concern and said: "Mom, are you OK?". I just said "No". I knew then that I had to make another difficult decision to leave this new job. On one hand, I felt like a failure, but on the other, I felt instantly freed when I made that decision. I committed to finishing out the calendar year with my employer and came up with a new plan.

In the new year, I started my own consulting company and wrote this book. I also got a part-time job as an academic tutor at a local elementary school and this helped me with purpose and belonging which I was desperately missing. I also really wanted to be creative again, as I was in the classroom. That role gave me all of those things and also allowed me to work with kids, something that, once again, I knew I missed desperately. I had the flexibility I needed with the part-time hours to do some consulting work as a professional development facilitator on SEL. Writing this book was a challenge I embraced with my growth mindset, and it has ended up being an incredibly rewarding experience. I was going through the storm to come out on the other end. It was messy and difficult but a truly valuable journey. My ability to make responsible decisions multiple times in the midst of it all was key to my ability to navigate this difficult time.

Being able to make sound decisions is a life skill. It's one we can get better at with time and practice. Experience helps us with this as well. The strategies and examples I have named here are a starting point. I know you'll grow your skills over time as you try to embrace some of these ideas. This work will help you move through the Confidence Zone into the Competence Zone.

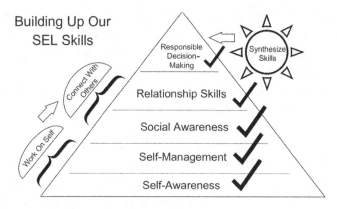

Figure 7.3 Building up our SEL skills.

 Reflection Questions

It's time to reflect on and process the information we are learning. Feel free to go back into the chapter to dig into some of these ideas. You can answer these questions by thinking about them, recording ideas in a journal, adding notes here, or creating audio or video notes.

TABLE 7.3 Link and QR code for the online reflection journal

I created an online tool with Google Jamboard that you can also access and use on your own if you'd like to. You can access it below. When you access the file, you'll be asked if you want to make a copy of the file. Say "yes" and this file will be in your Google Drive for you to use and refer back to throughout your reading of the text.		
Resource	**Link to Access**	**QR Code to Access**
"Embracing Adult SEL" Google Jamboard Reflection Journal	https://bit.ly/ EASELjournal5-8	

TABLE 7.4 Reflection activity: Responsible decision-making

What are some elements of Casel's definition of responsible decision-making? Share at least three ideas.		
Idea #1	**Idea #2**	**Idea #3**

TABLE 7.5 Reflection activity: Decision-making strategies

Choose three of the proactive strategies shared for responsible decision-making that you'd like to practice and embrace. What are they and why are you choosing them?		
Strategy #1	**Strategy #2**	**Strategy #3**
What?	What?	What?
Why?	Why?	Why?

TABLE 7.6 Reflection activity: Recent decisions

Reflect on two different decisions you made recently: one good one and one that was not ideal. Consider the elements of each one below and think about why it went well or not.
Recent good decision
Describe the situation.
How did it go well?
What will you do again in the future?
Recent poor decision
Describe the situation.
How did it go poorly?
What will you avoid in the future?

TABLE 7.7 Reflection activity: Recent decisions

We have all made great decisions in our personal and professional spaces. Take a moment to savor some good decisions you've made in your professional life recently.		
Great decision 1	**Great decision 2**	**Great decision 3**

8

Living Your Best SEL Life
Embrace SEL with Your Whole Self

"Hi Mom."

"I'm good, how are you doing?"

"Yes. Dan and the kids are good. Maggie is very excited to finish high school. Mike really likes his new workouts, and Dan is taking great care of us as always. Last night, he made us an awesome dinner of chicken parmesan. He tried a new homemade salad dressing recipe and it was delicious. I want to try to figure out how to make it, so I have it on hand when I need it. I finally got the patio cleaned up now that the pollen is pretty much done getting all over everything, and it's really lovely to sit out there. Bella likes it too and now is outside all the time."

"I am so sorry about this …. I feel awful telling you, but I'm not going to be able to make it to Grandpa's memorial service on Friday."

The words above are part of an actual phone conversation I had recently with my mom. "What?" you might say. Why on earth would I not attend my grandfather's memorial ceremony? I know this sounds like it doesn't make a lot of sense, but it did. At this moment, I was actually making a responsible decision. I was living in my social emotional learning (SEL) skills. Let me explain.

It was May. My grandfather had died the previous December. He was 93 years old and lived a full and long life. As my mom says, he got to do just about everything he wanted to. My grandpa was a hunter and carpenter in upstate New York. I have very fond memories of visits with him as a young child. We took snowmobile rides, dug up potatoes in the garden, and visited the mysterious "back room" where he skinned beaver and stored all of his hunting traps and gear. He fished, hunted deer, and had a camp with no electricity. It was really fun to visit! Our trips there were really important because this life was so different from our suburban childhood. It was really important to understand where our mother had come from, and we had gained perspective on life in small-town America. I shared the same birthday with him, April 9. Later in life, he wasn't able to do much as he slowed down, and when he died in late December, it was not much of a surprise. We celebrate Christmas and it would have been difficult to travel over four hours to the service that was held in his honor a few days before the holiday, with bad weather in the forecast. So it was decided there would be a burial and service to honor him in the spring.

Spring brought excitement in our family as our daughter was accepted to college and began to wrap up her high school career. At 18, our daughter was truly becoming an adult. Always an old soul, thoughtful and mature, she planned an amazing Mother's Day outing for us. Her favorite musician was coming to town and would play three shows over Mother's Day weekend. She was going with friends on Sunday night but had gotten us two tickets for Friday night; it would be a special mother-and-daughter outing. I was thrilled about the sentiment and excited for the show because I also loved the artist. I was truly touched by the idea that she wanted to spend the time with me.

Shortly after she got the tickets, we found out that my grandfather's burial and memorial service would be on the same day. Initially, I thought, no problem, I can do both. I would leave at 6 a.m., drive four and a half hours to make the 11 a.m. ceremony, spend two hours there, and drive back by 5:30 p.m. so we could go to the concert. This quick thinking and the belief that I am strong and capable had me thinking this was a good idea for several weeks. Dan immediately voiced concern over this scenario, but I assured him I could do it.

The week of the show arrived and I began to rethink everything. I started to get extremely nervous. First the drive. It would be nine hours of driving time if there was no traffic. Life experience has taught me that driving on a Friday in May would likely include traffic, especially in the busy northeast where we lived. A few weeks earlier, a trip up to New Jersey to visit my mom and sister for dinner had taken an hour longer than usual for this reason. Second, I realized that this would likely leave me exhausted when I got home for the show. My daughter and I would then drive to the concert, which would go until after 11 p.m. This would not leave me in good shape for the drive home, which could be unsafe. Additionally, if I encountered traffic on the way home from the memorial service, we could be late to the show.

My daughter would be devastated by this. Third, I wouldn't be my best self for our daughter, and she deserved the very best version of me for this special occasion: a happy, well-rested, not-stressed-out mom to enjoy the show with after spending a lot of time, effort, and money to get the tickets. It all started to not make very much sense, and I got worried but was also filled with terrible feelings over the idea of not going to the ceremony. My No. 1 concern was my mom and the idea that I would let her down. I also wanted to see my sister and my brother and many relatives I had not seen in a long time.

I thought it through again. I needed to make a decision. While calm and regulated, I referred to some of my key questions around decision-making and came to the conclusion that I would not attend the memorial after answering these questions.

TABLE 8.1 Questions in decision-making

Question	Answer
What are my options?	a. Attend memorial ceremony and potentially be late and exhausted for the concert b. Stay home and get to concert on time and be well rested but miss the memorial
What perspectives do I need to consider?	Most important: a. My daughter b. My mom
How can I stay safe?	Stay home and be well rested, prepared, and organized for the concert
Whom can I talk to?	a. My husband Dan b. My sister Tracy c. My mom

After answering all of these questions and talking to my husband and sister at length, I arrived at the decision that I needed to prioritize my relationship with our daughter and stay home so I could be well prepared to attend the concert. Both my husband and sister agreed that it was the right course of action. I just needed to tell my mom. I was nervous to make that phone call, but she immediately understood and told me that Maggie came first. I missed the burial and memorial ceremony, but I knew it was the correct thing to do. If I hadn't had the conflict of the plans with Maggie, I would have been there in a heartbeat, and I knew the people who needed to understand my decision did.

It ended up being the right decision. And it was a good thing I didn't try to be a superwoman and do both things. It took us two hours to get to the concert, which was only 25 miles away. The show went until after 11 p.m., and we sat in the parking lot for 75 minutes after the show because of the traffic. We got home close to 2 a.m. If I had attempted to do the long trip that day, I would have been in very rough shape for the show. As it played out, we had a very special memory together that I'll cherish forever, particularly as our daughter prepares to leave the nest and go to college in the fall.

I had made a responsible decision. I was living in SEL. I used my skills and navigated an everyday situation in an effective way. Although this was not easy, it worked. Even five years ago, I would probably not have approached this moment with the same calm and capable thinking that allowed me to get through it. I was undoubtedly better prepared to navigate this moment because of my Adult SEL skills.

What Does Living in SEL Look and Sound Like?

When we internalize the SEL competencies of self-awareness, self-management, social awareness, relationship skills, and responsible decision-making, we automatically live in them. We won't have to think about focusing on a skill and practicing it; it will happen in the moments we need them to in a seamless way. As we get better at these skills, we'll spend less energy thinking about them, what they are, and how to do them and more time just doing them. This will tax our Box of Energy less and leave it full to tackle other things in life. This will also happen in both our personal and professional lives. The last five years have taught me that this is holistic personal development. It would be very unlikely that I would start to do these things at school only and not at home and vice versa. This work has helped me become a more successful human being in the context of my various roles in life: educator, wife, friend, mom, co-worker, and more. I'm so grateful for this work and the growth that has come with it. In the garden of SEL, our skills and the positive benefits that come with them will blossom, bloom, and grow.

Time to Recap

Let's recall Casel's definition of SEL:

> *"SEL is the **process** through which all young people and adults **acquire and apply** the **knowledge, skills, and attitudes** to develop healthy identities, manage emotions and achieve personal and collective goals, feel and show empathy for others, establish and maintain supportive relationships, and make responsible and caring decisions."*

Here are key words and ideas:

> ★ It's a process. Process means "something going on" or "a series of action and operations" and "a phenomenon marked by gradual change leading to a result". By doing this work, you are engaging in a process that will allow you to be more successful in life both personally and professionally. This is the same thing we want for our students! We want them to be successful both in school and outside of it. Doing this work personally will trickle down into your professional life. Whether you are a classroom educator, teacher leader, or a school or district leader with positional authority, you'll see the benefits in your work life and you'll see them at home too.
>
> ★ We acquire and apply knowledge, skills, and mindsets that are part of SEL through this process. For me, it's always been fun and interesting to learn something new. From the time I stepped back into a classroom as a student in January 2006 through today, I have always enjoyed learning and embraced the idea of being a lifelong learner. The depth, complexity, and positive impact of working on these SEL skills will hopefully provide you with an opportunity to learn and grow. As we serve others in education, it is critically important that we take care of ourselves. I truly believe that engaging in positive growth is a way we can take care of ourselves.

I can see and feel evidence of growth in SEL skills all around me. It's happening with myself and my students because of the intention with which I bring it into the classroom and embrace it in my life. Sweet moments at home in SEL continue around me. The other morning, I came downstairs and the nail clipper was on the coffee table in the family room but no nail clippings were there. We celebrate Easter. When the holiday arrived this year, our son made waffles late at night and left them out as a surprise for all of us the next morning with a sticky note. The kitchen was cleaned up. My daughter asked me to do something one night and then said: "Never mind, we can look at this in the morning, it's not urgent right now". I smile inside at these moments.

Figure 8.1 Waffles on counter in clean kitchen.

More Than Self-Care

You may have noticed I haven't used the word self-care in this text. The concept of self-care is a valuable one. We all need to take care of ourselves in our personal and professional lives to move forward each day. That is clear. We need to do so in order to recover from work and be able to support the important people in our lives. However, in education, self-care has, at times, been weaponized against teachers. The idea that if teachers just "did self-care" they would be OK is a harmful one. At this moment in time, teachers are facing incredible levels of burnout due to the real demands of the job. In the wake of the Covid-19 pandemic, students have greater needs than in the past and fewer academic and social skills. In the effort to get back to normal, testing has resumed, and pacing guides and curriculum have changed very little, as has the very idea of school. The structure and demands of going to school have not evolved very much in spite of what has happened in the world. When a system doesn't look at the root causes of the need for significant amounts of self-care, that's a disservice to those in the system. Instead of focusing on self-care, I want to empower educators with ideas to foster SEL skill building. That's what this book is about: empowerment through explicit skill building.

One of my goals in writing this book was to create a resource for educators. I wanted to write a book that someone could read over the weekend and then be able to try some of the ideas in it on Monday. I also did not want to write another book on SEL in the classroom. There are many excellent resources on the market about how to do SEL with students and bring these skills and competencies alive in classrooms. By writing this book, I sought to create a tool that would help both educators and education leaders grow their personal SEL skills. I want to empower educators and education leaders with concrete, helpful, and impactful skills that enhance their personal and professional lives as well as the people around them. We know from research that Adult SEL is a requirement of successful SEL systems. I hope this book helps you grow your understanding through curiosity and learning and leads to the confidence to try out the skills that make sense for you and eventually builds your competence in SEL. My mission is to build curiosity, confidence, and competence in SEL.

My Best SEL Life Looks Like This

I love this famous education quote and go back to it often. It grounds me in my purpose and my power in a classroom. These often-referenced words come from Haim Ginott (1922–1973), a child psychologist and teacher from Israel:

> "I've come to a frightening conclusion that I am the decisive element in the classroom. It's my personal approach that creates the climate. It's my daily mood that makes the weather. As a teacher, I possess a tremendous power to make a child's life miserable or joyous. I can be a tool of torture or an instrument of inspiration. I can humiliate or heal. In all situations, it is my response that decides whether a crisis will be escalated or de-escalated and a child humanized or dehumanized."

When I reflect deeply on this quote, I am reminded of how critical SEL skills are in all facets of our lives, including the classroom. In our jobs in the classroom, where we live and breathe as humans, virtually every moment is on display for young people. Each young person we encounter has an idea of school that is directly related to the things we do and say, both to them and the others around us. It is therefore critical we build, hone, and maintain our SEL skills for everyday situations and model them in real time.

The word "mood" in the quote above is particularly powerful. For me, mood is tied to my self-awareness and self-management. When students experience bad moods, difficult emotions, or struggle, they can take advantage of calming spaces, cool-down routines, and specific interventions. As adults, often we don't have that luxury. There is no calm-down corner for teachers; we have to keep pushing through the moments that challenge us: the difficult ones, the heartbreaking ones, the frustrating ones, and the sad ones. This alone motivates me to work to continually build my SEL skills as when we can't manage what's happening, situations quickly become very difficult and can escalate to a place that won't work well for either us or our students. This negatively impacts learning.

Here are some ways I have been living my best SEL life. I'll highlight the competencies that match the personal and professional moments I share here.

Educator moment: self-awareness and self-management. I was organizing materials and supplies for a learning game for my students. I sometimes have eczema on my left hand. Eczema is rough, dry, scaly skin. It can flare during cold weather and is especially prone to show up on my ring finger. At times, it can be relieved with some creams and lotions; other times, it can be resistant and persist. On this day, it was pretty bad and my left hand looked ugly and raw with red scaly skin on the last two fingers. While I was passing out papers, a student saw it and yelled "Ew gross! Why does your hand look like that?" Other students heard this student and looked up at me. I immediately had lots of eyes on me and felt lots of tough emotions: shame, embarrassment, annoyance. While I was internally thinking about how annoying it was to be called out for something ugly I could not control, I also thought about the students' perspective; they had a point! My hand did look terrible. So I paused, took a breath, and then asked that student to hand out the pencils to direct their energy elsewhere. I continued handing out papers so my students could see me manage the moment, not respond negatively to those hurtful words. The session then continued well.

Family moment: self-awareness and self-management. Everyone once in a while, I ask our kids to bring any cups, plates, bowls, bottles, and utensils down from their rooms and up from the basement to the kitchen. I find that, without reminders, teenagers will rarely do this on their own. I am well aware of my annoyance around this. One day recently, our son did this for me right before we went to school. I drove him to school and got back home and realized he just threw everything into the sink. It was full of water bottles without the caps, small bowls, and a few plates. I actually counted TEN water bottles!! I immediately started to think about how I was frustrated that he did not load everything into the dishwasher. However, I instantly reframed the situation. He was well hydrated and was in the habit of drinking lots of water!

And he brought everything down when I asked him to. That was it. It happened instantly without a lot of thought. I got a smile on my face and loaded the dishwasher. I also realized that if I wanted the items to be loaded into the dishwasher, I would have to ask specifically for that to be done. He had, after all, complied with my request, which was to bring everything to the kitchen.

Educator moment: social awareness. It was the first day of the holy month of Ramadan. One of my students was wearing a long robe at school. I complimented her and she let me know she was wearing it was for Ramadan. I told her it was beautiful. She then asked me if we were going to watch any videos with music in them during class that day. I said I would check and asked if she would mind telling me why. She explained that for the first day of the holy month of Ramadan, she could not listen to music and would leave the classroom if needed. I checked my plans and changed the video we were going to watch. I did not want her to have to leave the classroom, so I made sure the activities were inclusive and respected her culture and traditions.

Friend moment: social awareness. It was Passover. I looked up the Hebrew greeting for the holiday and sent a text message, using the traditional language, to several friends who were celebrating.

Educator moments: social awareness and relationship skills. Over the years, students and families have asked if they could share their culture, customs, holidays, and family stories with our class. I always say yes and invite people in to teach students about their experiences and knowledge. Here are a few examples:

> ★ A student wanted to teach our class about the Hindu harvest festival of Pongal. She prepared a Google Slides presentation and shared it with the class. Everyone loved it and she glowed with joy and confidence.
> ★ A student had been adopted from China. The family came into class to share the adoption story, teach students about the geography and culture of China, and prepared a snack of Chinese dumplings for all of us.
> ★ A parent and sibling joined our class to teach the students about their family traditions in celebrating Hanukkah, the Jewish festival of lights, in December.
> ★ A parent who was born in Taiwan came in to teach the class about Chinese New Year. The lesson included songs, a parade around the school carrying a red dragon, and a snack of fried rice.
> ★ A parent who is an artist joined our class for an art lesson and helped students create a project for Valentine's Day to take home and enjoy with their families.

> ★ A parent who is a physical therapist came in to teach children about their skeletal system and helped students build a model of their bones with Play-Doh.
> ★ A parent joined our class to teach students about Diwali, the Hindu festival of lights, and prepared a snack that contained cardamom, a spice commonly used in Indian food.

Family moment: relationship skills. Each day around dinner time, my husband and I sit down to chat. We do this on the living room or out on the patio when we can. We just ask how the day was and if anything interesting happened, and we check in with what is going on. It's a 30-minute ritual that keeps us connected. Some nights are filled with lively conversation, others are quieter. Some are interrupted by kids, phone calls, or something else. But we always make the effort, and the power of this ritual for our connection is clear. We miss it when we can't do it. It's now automatic and helps keep our connection strong even as the demands of everyday life surround us and time marches on.

Educator moment: responsible decision-making and relationship skills. Each week, I prepare a summary newsletter to send to families on Fridays. When I began teaching, I prepared a paper version and emailed out a PDF document. Now I use Adobe Spark and create a web page and share a link that can be easily accessed on a phone or laptop. This is a fun and easy way to share our classroom happenings with families. An accountability piece for me, it helps me to recap our week and review what we learned and did in each subject area as well with respect to SEL. At times, it's a wake-up call for me because I realized I did not get to a certain activity or cover a topic the way I wanted to. I add photos of kids working and playing together throughout the week and resources for parents, such as articles and videos that might be helpful. Although this takes at least an hour to do and might be viewed as extra work, I view it as an investment into the relationships I have with my families. Over the years, they have let me know they can't wait to receive the newsletter every Friday. They love the pictures, and some families save the link each week as a memory.

Family moment: self-management. I am an organized person. I like to keep things neat and tidy around the house and generally in my life. Sometimes, things could be cleaner, but they are in order. I think this stems from my childhood. When our family was in disarray and my parents were getting divorced, I think I wanted things neat on the outside to hide the pain, messiness, and disarray that was on the inside when things were falling apart. When one of our kids gets home, they always leave everything – including a water bottle, keys, lanyard, receipts, change, and books – right on the kitchen counter, which is the first place you see when you walk in. The backpack is on the floor, where you can trip over it. This annoys me greatly, so I immediately act and reframe. If the child is nearby, I ask them to take care of things and they will gladly do it. If they are not, I just move things to hooks and doorknobs as needed. I know that soon I'll miss this evidence of our child being safe and well at home, so I'm trying to actually savor it and reframe and enjoy those everyday items being in my way.

Educator moment: responsible decision-making. When I can, I highlight for my students which SEL skills we will specifically practice when we do a learning activity. I list out the exact skills we need to use to be successful, and I go over them before we start a learning sequence. Below is an example of how we talked about SEL before a math activity. The slide you see here is the actual slide I shared in my classroom before learning together.

Example
Math Warm-up - Measurement On the Playground

MATH Skills	Social Emotional Learning

1. **Using Math Tool**
   a. meter stick
 2. **Measuring large items**
   a. playground
 3. **Recording Data**
   a. Use data sheet
   b. Take turns in roles
	1. **Relationship Skills**
	   a. Listening
	   b. Using kind words
	 2. **Responsible Decision-Making**
	   a. Appropriate use of tools
	   b. Follow protocol
	 3. **Self-Management**
	   a. Staying in learning brain
	   b. Staying on task

Figure 8.2 Classroom example of integrating academic and SEL skills.

Family moment: self-management and relationship skills. After lots of trial and error, I don't try to talk to our teenage kids if they don't want to. I wait. It helps me avoid annoyance and unnecessary arguments. Although this can be annoying, I just work through it. A part of me wants to just say "why do I need to be on your schedule or emotional timetable instead of mine", but then I realize my job as a parent is to be present and available for our kids. This decision brings this back into focus and makes a positive difference.

Human moment: relationship skills. We all have gotten gifts we don't love. Some can be easily passed on and forgotten but some matter. For those people who are important in my life, I save the gift to use or wear it when I see them, so they know they are important to me. This could be a piece of jewelry or clothing or a serving dish. Whatever the case, this is a very small and easy way to pour into the relationship.

Family moment: self-management. Our daughter was at a party and asked to be picked up at 7:15 p.m. I got there right on time and texted her to let her know I was there. She told me she was still talking to some people, and would it be OK if she stayed a little while longer? I immediately said yes, no problem. I could have been annoyed about the wait time, but I reframed the moment to focus on the fact that she was having fun socializing. I read some articles I had been saving in my email on my phone while I waited about 30 more minutes. She came out smiling and told me all about the party. It was so worth it to wait calmly and patiently and not focus on the small inconvenience. I was happy and regulated and so was she. It was a win all around.

Educator moment: responsible decision-making. I'm so grateful for my friend Stephanie. We worked together when I left the classroom and she was such an incredible source of support and inspiration. She shared her plans with me one day and told me about the "2 cents conversation" protocol. She was going to use it with her students. After she briefly explained that it was a way to foster discussion and ensure equity of voice, I was intrigued. I learned about it with resources she shared with me and then tried it out myself. Since then, I have used it with adults and students with great success. In a recent professional development session I was facilitating on SEL, I shared the strategy and had the participants engage in the protocol themselves so they could not only learn about it but take it right back to their classrooms. When I reflected on it, I realized this simple protocol really supported all five SEL competencies. When using it, people need to think about their own thoughts and feelings, manage themselves well to stay in accordance with the protocol, and listen to the ideas and perspectives of others. This would enhance their relationships with the other participants. They would also have to make the decision to engage in the discussion in the format presented. What a powerful way to integrate SEL into academics. You can learn more about this discussion protocol here.

TABLE 8.2 Link and QR code for put your two cents in

Resource	Bitly Link to Access	QR Code to Access
Video: *"Put Your Two Cents In"*	https://bit.ly/EASELput	

I could go on and on with more examples like these. I know as you grow your skills you'll be able to identify countless moments like these that are evidence of your work in SEL and your effectiveness with your growing skills.

Using Casel's "3 Signature Practices" in the Classroom

As you can see by now, lots of your SEL skills and practices will trickle down into the classroom and school environment as you live and work each day. As you work to increase your skills, they will become a part of your whole self. Still, you may have questions about how to incorporate and integrate SEL into your classroom effectively. Using Casel's "3 Signature Practices" is a great way to bring SEL into the classroom without formal curriculum. These are the signature practices:

> ★ Welcoming inclusion activities
> ★ Engaging strategies, brain breaks, and transitions
> ★ Optimistic closures

It's been a very responsible decision for me to incorporate these practices into my classroom and the professional development sessions I create and deliver. The difference that embracing these practices has produced has been profoundly positive! My own interpretation of each practice is below:

Welcoming inclusion activities. Each one of us wants to feel welcome in the spaces we occupy. In my experience, we often need transition time and space at the beginning of activities. This is especially true for children of all ages whom we ask to transition often and quickly throughout the day. Taking the time to offer a check-in, a round-up activity, or even quiet time to get ready to begin learning together is incredibly important. I have used inclusive welcoming activities at the beginning of the school day, college classes, virtual meetings, and short learning sessions such as a 30-minute group lesson. They are welcome and successful all the time! People of all ages love to start with a smile, sharing and joy. These rituals are part of my practice and are now a non-negotiable element of my work as an educator, no matter whom I am working with. Here are a few ideas for you to consider embracing:

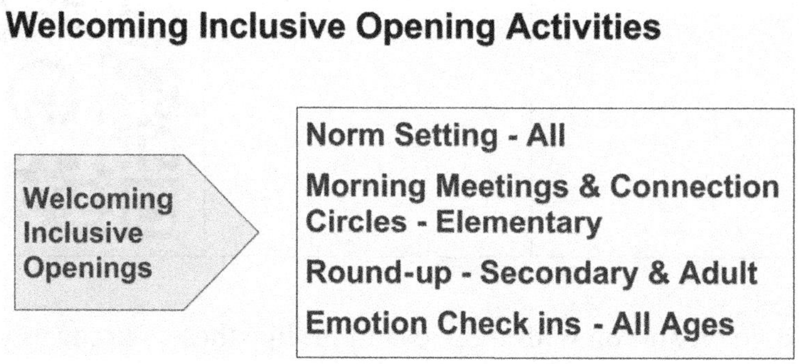

Welcoming Inclusive Opening Activities

Welcoming Inclusive Openings →
- Norm Setting - All
- Morning Meetings & Connection Circles - Elementary
- Round-up - Secondary & Adult
- Emotion Check ins - All Ages

Figure 8.3 Welcoming inclusive activities.

All of these activities should be inclusive, joyful, connecting, organized, safe, and authentic and ensure equity of voice. When you consider all of these elements, you'll see really incredible sharing, and the result will be a strong community of learners who are ready to take risks and grow together. I couldn't teach or run effective professional development without this practice. I also recommend the use of a talking piece to help things run smoothly and effectively and with equity of voice.

Engaging strategies, brain breaks, and transitions. As we spend time leading students in learning, it's critically important to invest in regulation. So much of student behavior is tied up in how we structure and manage our classrooms and learning environments. Incorporating really engaging learning strategies, lots of brain breaks, and productive transitions is key. As with my welcoming and inclusive activities I begin with in the first practice, I utilize this practice in both my learning with students of all ages and adult professional development sessions I facilitate. Attending to this practice with great effort yields great results! Here are some key ideas and questions to consider.

With engagement strategies, I like to ask myself a few questions as I plan to hold myself accountable for creating compelling, fun, and exciting learning experiences. These questions are essential for both students and adult learners:

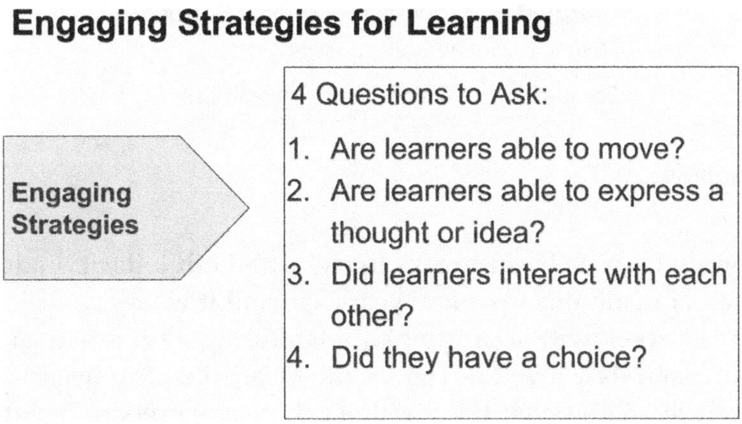

Engaging Strategies for Learning

Engaging Strategies →

4 Questions to Ask:
1. Are learners able to move?
2. Are learners able to express a thought or idea?
3. Did learners interact with each other?
4. Did they have a choice?

Figure 8.4 Strategies for engagement.

Generally, I find that when learners can move, it stimulates excitement and engagement. When people can safely express a thought or idea about their learning or a topic, they feel seen, heard, and validated. Adding choice as well as an element of being social is helpful as well. No one, myself included, wants to sit and listen for long periods of time. I think about how I would feel in my own learning experience, and if it's bored or unengaged, I work to change the plan. Now these questions are automatically incorporated into my plans on a regular basis; they are second nature to me.

When I started teaching, I rarely used formal brain breaks. I had never learned about them in my preparation program. Brain breaks are now a staple of my planning, and I use them on a regular basis with both students and adult learners. As with the other practices, I think there are different types of brain breaks to consider and key questions to ask when planning to use them. I like to classify brain breaks into different categories and use them at different parts of the day as needed, and I always work to read my audience to see if I need to interject the room with an activity to stimulate learning. Several different types of brain breaks are shown below. With practice, you'll understand what your students or audience may need at a particular moment and develop effective strategies.

Brain Breaks - Variety, Attunement Key

Energy Up - Go Noodle Fun, UJU YouTube, Rock Paper Scissors Tournament

Creating - 5 minutes with Play-Doh, Legos, Small puzzles

Energy Down - Journaling, Mindful Coloring, Cosmic Kids YouTube, Box Breathing

Connections - Quick Chats, Walk & Talk

Figure 8.5 Brain breaks.

One of my favorite brain breaks to use with both kids and adults is the "quick chat". I made this up a few years ago and it works so well. In fact, I just did it last week with a group of adults during a professional development session and they loved it. Here is the idea. Find a connection question and let your learners know the question. (I always prepare a slide to help facilitate this activity.) Then ask them to get up, walk around, and find a partner to talk about the question for one minute. When they hear the chime, they find a new partner to chat with. Do this for five rounds of one minute each. The vibe is positive and fun, people are moving and connecting, and it takes only five minutes. It's such a great way to boost energy and create connections.

"Quick Chat" Conversation Time

I'll share a question.

When I ring the chime, find someone in the class to answer the question with. Both of you should share your answer with the other person. You have 1 minute.

When the chime rings again, find a new person and do it again.

Have fun chatting with 5 different people.

©2023 Wendy Turner Consulting, LLC. Not for Reproduction/Distribution.

Figure 8.6 "Quick chat" brain break.

Optimistic closures. Finally, we can use optimistic closures to help us end on a positive note. This again is a practice that I just can't imagine teaching without. On the very worst of days, after the hardest of situations, we can identify something good so we close on a positive note. Again, I use this practice with learners of all ages, from elementary school to college students as well as in the professional development sessions I develop and run. I started using this practice during remote learning with my second graders. I created a predictable schedule of positive closures that remained the same each day of the week so students knew what was coming each day and could gather their thoughts to share:

Optimistic Closures: Ending on a Positive Note

★ Monday: What went well?
★ Tuesday: 3 Good Things
★ Wednesday: 3As - Appreciation, Apology, Aha
★ Thursday - Shout-outs
★ Friday - What are you looking forward to?

Figure 8.7 Optimistic closures.

For single-session professional development as well as Mondays, I use the simple question "What went well?" with my learners. This is a question that everyone can usually answer fairly easily. People can build on each other's ideas or even share the same idea. It helps us to focus on the good. Similarly, on Tuesdays in my classroom, I ask students to identify "3 Good Things". This positivity practice asks everyone to name three good things from their day; they can be focused on home, school, academics, lunch and recess, or relationships. I love to see students evolve over time to be able to answer this question with ease after it stumps them a bit when we start. On Wednesdays, we move to a more thoughtful closing that ask students to share an appreciation for someone, an "aha" moment in their learning, or an apology for someone they need to repair with. It's wonderful to be able to create a simple opportunity for students to work on their relationships with each other during a seemingly innocuous closing activity. On Thursdays, we pivot to shout-outs: students can shout out someone in the classroom for being a good friend or assisting with work during the day or congratulating them for doing well. Some of the most powerful shout-outs I have observed over the years involve students complimenting each other for getting through tough emotions. They are watching and learning from each other all the time. On Fridays, we round out the week by sharing something we are looking forward to; this works well with the coming weekend but can also be a longer-term view. Some students share that they will miss the classroom community over our time apart and look forward to being back together next week.

However you choose to embrace and implement the 3 Signature Practices, I wish you well with them! They have forever changed the way I teach and facilitate learning in my classrooms and professional development sessions. Quite simply, I can't teach without them. This is an effective and relatively easy way to bring SEL into your learning space.

A Final Note

The last several months have been an incredible journey for me and a very real part of the process of writing this book. After lots of complicated emotions, ups and downs, and deep thinking and reflection, I'm happy to share that I will most likely return to the classroom this year. My decision to leave was never about the people around me. I have worked for many years with so many incredible, talented, and selfless educators and staff who are, quite simply, incredible human beings. They are powerful models of excellence for me in so many ways. I have learned so much from all of them. I realize now I just needed a break. I am also thrilled beyond measure to have been able to write this book, which I hope will be a valuable and helpful resource for educators. Will it solve all of our problems? Absolutely not. But can the ideas, skills, and strategies here help in various ways? It is my deep and sincere hope that this is the case.

When I return, I'll embrace my role with all of my SEL skills firmly in place. This will benefit me and my students enormously. I'll once again enjoy working with kids, being part of a community, and being creative with my craft – all the things I desperately missed while I was away from the classroom. I'll safeguard my physical and mental health with great ferocity so I can avoid burnout in the future. I will no longer provide professional development for free, and I'll leave on time. I hope you do too. I know my SEL skills will help me with this, and yours will help you to do it as well. You are now empowered with specific SEL skills.

Congratulations! You have learned so much in your journey toward competence in SEL. I am proud of you and your investment in this critical component of education and life. I'd love to hear from you: what's working, what you have questions with, and some of the everyday moments that stop you in your tracks for either good or bad reasons. Please reach out via email (wendy@wendyturnerconsulting.com) or find me on social media to share.

This book is really a love letter to educators. I see you. I see the extraordinary amount of your heart and soul that you pour into your students and your work. I see how challenging things have been over the last few years and continue to be. This resource is meant to empower you so that you can learn skills that will help you to be more successful in your personal and professional life. If it's helpful, please share it with someone else. I wish you all the best going forward!

Reflection Questions

It's time to reflect on and process the information we are learning. Feel free to go back into the chapter to dig into some of these ideas. You can answer these questions by thinking about them, recording ideas in a journal, adding notes here, or creating audio or video notes.

TABLE 8.3 Link and QR code for the online reflection journal

I created an online tool with Google Jamboard that you can also access and use on your own if you'd like to. You can access it below. When you access the file, you'll be asked if you want to make a copy of the file. Say "yes" and this file will be in your Google Drive for you to use and refer back to throughout your reading of the text.		
Resource	**Bitly Link to Access**	**QR Code to Access**
"Embracing Adult SEL" Google Jamboard Reflection Journal	https://bit.ly/EASELjournal5-8	

TABLE 8.4 Reflection activity: Biggest takeaways

What are your three biggest takeaways from reading this book?		
Idea #1	**Idea #2**	**Idea #3**

TABLE 8.5 Reflection activity: "3 Signature Practices"

Describe Casel's "3 Signature Practices". What is one way you'll implement each idea into your learning space?		
Practice #1	**Practice #2**	**Practice #3**
What?	What?	What?
How?	How?	How?

TABLE 8.6 Reflection activity: Best SEL life

Identify two ways you have been living your best SEL life recently.
Recent real-life SEL moment
Recent real-life SEL moment

References

Chapter 1

Advancing Social and emotional learning. CASEL. (2023, May 1). https://casel.org/

Collins, M. (2022). *Your teacher leadership journey: A blueprint for growth and success.* Routledge, Taylor & Francis Group.

Fundamentals of sel. CASEL. (2022, March 11). https://casel.org/fundamentals-of-sel/

Home. Edutopia. (n.d.). https://www.edutopia.org/

Institute, T. S. (2021, August 18). *"SEL is the heartbeat of the classroom." TSI's founder @soLaur kicks off the #winatsocial summit highlighting words of wisdom from former Delaware teacher of the year, @mrswendymturner PIC.TWITTER.COM/J8KC5HF2ED.* Twitter. https://twitter.com/TheSocialInst/status/1428040771303772163

McClure, B. M. (2020, May 18). *Why every school must have a social emotional learning plan prior to reopening.* Lessons for SEL. https://bit.ly/EASELwhy

McClure, B. M. (2022, September 30). *Did you know that SEL emerged because of a black man? the true history of SEL.* Lessons for SEL. https://www.lessonsforsel.com/post/did-you-know-that-sel-emerged-because-of-a-black-man-the-true-history-of-sel

Merriam-Webster. (n.d.-a). Emotional. In Merriam-Webster.com dictionary. Retrieved May 22, 2023, from https://www.merriam-webster.com/dictionary/emotional

Merriam-Webster. (n.d.-b). Learning. In Merriam-Webster.com dictionary. Retrieved May 22, 2023, from https://www.merriam-webster.com/dictionary/learning

Merriam-Webster. (n.d.-c). Social. In Merriam-Webster.com dictionary. Retrieved May 22, 2023, from https://www.merriam-webster.com/dictionary/social

Obama, M. (2022). *Light we carry.* Crown.

Preparing teachers to support social and emotional learning. Learning Policy Institute. (2022, August 26). https://learningpolicyinstitute.org/product/social-and-emotional-learning-case-study-san-jose-state-report

Prothero, A. (2023, January 4). *What does SEL mean anyway? 7 experts break it down.* Education Week.

Reilly, K. (2022, April 27). *What is social and emotional learning? The New School Target*. Time. https://time.com/6170755/social-emotional-learning-schools-conservative-backlash/

SEL 3 signature practices playbook. SEL 3 Signature Practices Playbook - Casel Schoolguide. (n.d.). https://schoolguide.casel.org/resource/three-signature-sel-practices-for-the-classroom/

Social Emotional Learning: Not just for kids. Cult of Pedagogy. (2021, October 8). https://www.cultofpedagogy.com/sel-adults/

Teaching SEL during covid: Lessons learned and three tips for educators moving forward. The Social Institute. (2021, July 26). https://thesocialinstitute.com/blog/teaching-sel-during-covid-lessons-learned-and-three-tips-for-educators-moving-forward/

What does the research say? CASEL. (2022, May 26). https://casel.org/fundamentals-of-sel/what-does-the-research-say/

YouTube. (n.d.). *Lessons for Sel*. YouTube. https://www.youtube.com/@lessonsforsel9397

Chapter 2

Leader in me. Leader in Me. (n.d.). https://www.leaderinme.com/

Merriam-Webster. (n.d.-a). Proactive. In Merriam-Webster.com dictionary. Retrieved May 22, 2023, from https://www.merriam-webster.com/dictionary/proactive

Merriam-Webster. (n.d.-b). Moment. In Merriam-Webster.com dictionary. Retrieved May 22, 2023, from https://www.merriam-webster.com/dictionary/moment

Merriam-Webster. (n.d.-c). Reflection. In Merriam-Webster.com dictionary. Retrieved May 22, 2023, from https://www.merriam-webster.com/dictionary/reflection

Chapter 3

Adams, H. K. (2022, March 3). *How to use an identity wheel to have better conversations about diversity*. Fairygodboss. https://fairygodboss.com/career-topics/identity-wheel#

Deak, J. M., & Ackerley, S. (2017). *Your fantastic elastic brain: Stretch it, shape it*. Little Pickle Press.

Fundamentals of sel. CASEL. (2022, March 11). https://casel.org/fundamentals-of-sel/

Hammond, Z. (2015). *Culturally responsive teaching and the brain: Promoting authentic engagement and rigor among culturally and linguistically diverse students.* Corwin, a SAGE Company.

Implicit bias: Concepts unwrapped. YouTube. (2018, October 31). https://youtu.be/OoBvzI-YZf4

McClure, B., & Reed, K. (2022). *Hacking deficit thinking: 8 reframes that will change the way you think about strength-based practices and equity in schools.* Times 10 Publications.

Merriam-Webster. (n.d.-a). Awareness. In Merriam-Webster.com dictionary. Retrieved May 22, 2023, from https://www.merriam-webster.com/dictionary/awareness

Merriam-Webster. (n.d.-b). Identity. In Merriam-Webster.com dictionary. Retrieved May 22, 2023, from https://www.merriam-webster.com/dictionary/identity

Merriam-Webster. (n.d.-c). Implicit bias. In Merriam-Webster.com dictionary. Retrieved May 22, 2023, from https://www.merriam-webster.com/dictionary/implicit%20bias

Merriam-Webster. (n.d.-d). Mindset. In Merriam-Webster.com dictionary. Retrieved May 22, 2023, from https://www.merriam-webster.com/dictionary/mindset

Merriam-Webster. (n.d.-e). Self. In Merriam-Webster.com dictionary. Retrieved May 22, 2023, from https://www.merriam-webster.com/dictionary/self

Projectimplicit. Project Implicit. (n.d.). https://implicit.harvard.edu/implicit/

Scott, E. (2022, November 14). *The differences between Optimists and pessimists.* Verywell Mind. https://www.verywellmind.com/the-benefits-of-optimism-3144811

Sussex Publishers. (n.d.). *6 ways to discover and Choose your core values.* Psychology Today. https://www.psychologytoday.com/us/blog/change-power/201811/6-ways-discover-and-choose-your-core-values

Turner, W. (2022, August 31). *"Where I'm from" Writing activity.* Fresh Ideas for Teaching. https://blog.savvas.com/where-im-from-writing-activity/

Via Character Strengths Survey & Character Reports. VIA Institute on Character. (n.d.). https://www.viacharacter.org/

Where I'm from, a poem by George Ella Lyon, writer and teacher. (n.d.). http://www.georgeellalyon.com/where.html

YouTube. (2017, August 24). *Brain 101 | National Geographic.* YouTube. https://www.youtube.com/watch?v=pRFXSjkpKWA

Chapter 4

American Psychological Association. (n.d.). *Nurtured by nature.* Monitor on Psychology. https://www.apa.org/monitor/2020/04/nurtured-nature

Blum, D. (2021, May 4). *The other side of languishing is flourishing. Here's how to get there.* The New York Times. https://www.nytimes.com/2021/05/04/well/mind/flourishing-languishing.html

Fundamentals of sel. CASEL. (2022, March 11). https://casel.org/fundamentals-of-sel/

Heggart, K. (2015, February 4). *Developing a growth mindset in teachers and staff.* Edutopia. https://www.edutopia.org/discussion/developing-growth-mindset-teachers-and-staff

Kinds of kindness - empatico. The Great Empatico Expedition. (n.d.). https://expedition.empatico.org/activities/kinds-of-kindness?lng=en

Kumar, K. (2021, November 18). *Why do Navy seals use box breathing? 4 benefits, 4 steps.* MedicineNet. https://www.medicinenet.com/why_do_navy_seals_use_box_breathing/article.htm

Merriam-Webster. (n.d.-a). Affective. In Merriam-Webster.com dictionary. Retrieved May 22, 2023, from https://www.merriam-webster.com/dictionary/affective

Merriam-Webster. (n.d.-b). Judgment. In Merriam-Webster.com dictionary. Retrieved May 22, 2023, from https://www.merriam-webster.com/dictionary/judgment

Merriam-Webster. (n.d.-c). Kindness. In Merriam-Webster.com dictionary. Retrieved July 31, 2023, from https://www.merriam-webster.com/dictionary/kind

Merriam-Webster. (n.d.-d). Management. In Merriam-Webster.com dictionary. Retrieved May 22, 2023, from https://www.merriam-webster.com/dictionary/management

Merriam-Webster. (n.d.-e). Self. In Merriam-Webster.com dictionary. Retrieved May 22, 2023, from https://www.merriam-webster.com/dictionary/self

Merriam-Webster. (n.d.-f). Statement. In Merriam-Webster.com dictionary. Retrieved May 22, 2023, from https://www.merriam-webster.com/dictionary/statement

Muhammad, A.-M. (2019). *The restorative journey.* Akoben.

Paul, A. M. (2022). *The extended mind: The power of thinking outside the brain.* Mariner Books.

Social Emotional Learning: Not just for kids. Cult of pedagogy. (2021, October 8). https://www.cultofpedagogy.com/sel-adults/

Souers, K., & Hall, P. A. (2016). *Fostering resilient learners: Strategies for creating a trauma-sensitive classroom*. Hawker Brownlow Education.

Suttie, J. S. J. (n.d.). *How kindness fits into a happy life*. Greater Good. https://greatergood.berkeley.edu/article/item/how_kindness_fits_into_a_happy_life

Turner, W. (2020, March 5). *Rubber bracelets to support emotional regulation? Absolutely!*. Fostering Resilient Learners. https://www.fosteringresilientlearners.org/blog/2019/4/8/rubber-bracelets-to-support-emotional-regulation-absolutely

Turner, W. (2022, August 1). *3 good things: Positive practice for educators*. Fresh Ideas for Teaching. https://blog.savvas.com/3-good-things-positive-practice-for-educators/

WebMD. (n.d.). *Box breathing: Getting started with box breathing, how to do it, benefits and tips*. WebMD. https://www.webmd.com/balance/what-is-box-breathing

Chapter 5

Cherry, K. (2023, January 23). *How othering contributes to discrimination and Prejudice*. Verywell Mind. https://www.verywellmind.com/what-is-othering-5084425

December can be tough. let's bring empathy and Grace into our schools in the New Year. Home. (n.d.). https://www.edpost.com/stories/december-was-tough-so-im-bringing-empathy-and-grace-to-my-classroom-in-the-new-year

Fundamentals of sel. CASEL. (2022, March 11). https://casel.org/fundamentals-of-sel/

Gray, J., & Thomas, H. (2005). *If she only knew me*. Rocket Pub.

How opening up to my colleagues made me realize social-emotional learning isn't just for students. Home. (n.d.). https://www.edpost.com/stories/how-opening-up-to-my-colleagues-made-me-realize-social-emotional-learning-isnt-just-for-students

Merriam-Webster. (n.d.-a). Awareness. In Merriam-Webster.com dictionary. Retrieved May 22, 2023, from https://www.merriam-webster.com/dictionary/awareness

Merriam-Webster. (n.d.-b). Empathy. In Merriam-Webster.com dictionary. Retrieved May 22, 2023, from https://www.merriam-webster.com/dictionary/empathy

Merriam-Webster. (n.d.-c). Other. In Merriam-Webster.com dictionary. Retrieved May 22, 2023, from https://www.merriam-webster.com/dictionary/other

Merriam-Webster. (n.d.-d). Social. In Merriam-Webster.com dictionary. Retrieved May 22, 2023, from https://www.merriam-webster.com/dictionary/social

Morin, A. (2021, April 6). *7 ways to show empathy to students*. Understood. https://www.understood.org/en/articles/7-ways-to-respond-to-students-with-empathy

Venet, A. S. (2018, November 8). *A simple but powerful class opening activity*. Edutopia. https://www.edutopia.org/article/simple-powerful-class-opening-activity/

Chapter 6

Brené Brown on empathy. YouTube. (2013, December 10). https://youtu.be/1Evwgu369Jw

Fundamentals of sel. CASEL. (2022, March 11). https://casel.org/fundamentals-of-sel/

Merriam-Webster. (n.d.-a). Relationship. In Merriam-Webster.com dictionary. Retrieved May 22, 2023, from https://www.merriam-webster.com/dictionary/relationship

Merriam-Webster. (n.d.-b). Skill. In Merriam-Webster.com dictionary. Retrieved May 22, 2023, from https://www.merriam-webster.com/dictionary/skill

Thiel, M. (2020, April 17). *Story #3: A Car // a conversation // a connection*. Story #3: A Car // A Conversation // A Connection. https://humanconnectionchronicles.blogspot.com/2020/04/story-3-car-conversation-connection.html

YouTube. (2013, February 19). *How to be a good listener*. YouTube. https://www.youtube.com/watch?v=8XUE3urz3Fc

Chapter 7

Adelman, M. (2023, March 8). *When's the best time of day to make a decision?* HowStuffWorks Science. https://science.howstuffworks.com/life/inside-the-mind/human-brain/whens-the-best-time-day-make-a-decision.htm

Empatico I Connect Your Classroom to the world. (n.d.). https://edu.empatico.org/login

Fundamentals of sel. CASEL. (2022, March 11). https://casel.org/fundamentals-of-sel/

Merriam-Webster. (n.d.-a). Decision. In Merriam-Webster.com dictionary. Retrieved May 22, 2023, from https://www.merriam-webster.com/dictionary/decision

Merriam-Webster. (n.d.-b). Making. In Merriam-Webster.com dictionary. Retrieved May 22, 2023, from https://www.merriam-webster.com/dictionary/making

Merriam-Webster. (n.d.-c). Responsible. In Merriam-Webster.com dictionary. Retrieved May 22, 2023, from https://www.merriam-webster.com/dictionary/responsible

The sunk cost fallacy. The Decision Lab. (n.d.). https://thedecisionlab.com/biases/the-sunk-cost-fallacy

YouTube. (2020, April 16). *Empatico Empathy Hour with Wendy Turner*. YouTube. https://www.youtube.com/watch?v=zRiIJwvDEFc

Chapter 8

Fundamentals of SEL. CASEL. (2022, March 11). https://casel.org/fundamentals-of-sel/

Goodreads. (n.d.-a). *A quote by Haim G. Ginott*. Goodreads. https://www.goodreads.com/quotes/81938-i-ve-come-to-a-frightening-conclusion-that-i-am-the

Goodreads. (n.d.-b). *Haim G. Ginott (author of between parent and child)*. Goodreads. https://www.goodreads.com/author/show/212291.Haim_G_Ginott

Person. (2018, August 10). *60-second strategy: Appreciation, apology, aha!*. Edutopia. https://www.edutopia.org/video/60-second-strategy-appreciation-apology-aha

Put your two cents in - CLR discussion protocol. YouTube. (2016, September 9). https://youtu.be/VTpa0eWQfko

SEL 3 signature practices playbook - Casel schoolguide. (n.d.). https://schoolguide.casel.org/uploads/2018/12/CASEL_SEL-3-Signature-Practices-Playbook-V3.pdf

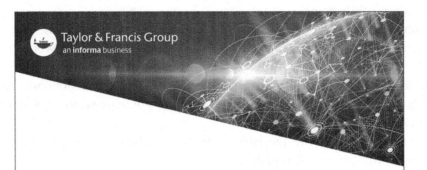

Made in the USA
Monee, IL
28 February 2025

13125711R00116